About the

Andy Elleray has been working in the goalkeeping world since the age of 14 and playing in goal since the age of seven. Over the years, his goalkeeping passion has seen him represent England's Blind Football team playing as the sighted goalkeeper as well as working at such clubs as Liverpool and Chelsea in a goalkeeping capacity. He has studied coaching and performance analysis for many years and has a Master's degree in Sports Coaching along with high level FA and UEFA qualifications.

Andy released his first book – *Scientific Approaches to Goalkeeping in Football* – in March 2013 and it aimed to invoke innovative thinking behind the position and investigate areas such as psychology, biomechanics, performance analysis and practice strictures amongst others. With selected exercises taken from his first book, *65 Goalkeeper Training Exercises* was published in 2017 and promotes different games within a goalkeeping environment in a quick and easy format.

Over the past five years, Andy has been working in Women's football as Head of Goalkeeping Development at Birmingham City Ladies alongside the women's international age group teams and the regional excellence pathway – while also holding a position as academy goalkeeping coach at the boy's side of the club.

Cancer Research

The author royalties from this book will go to Cancer Research.

Cancer Research UK is a cancer research and awareness charity in the United Kingdom formed, in 2002, by the merger of The Cancer Research Campaign and the Imperial Cancer Research Fund. Its aim is to reduce the number of deaths from cancer. As the world's largest independent cancer research charity, it conducts research into the prevention, diagnosis, and treatment of the disease.

Over recent months, I've experienced the effects of cancer first-hand as our first team goalkeeper at Birmingham City Ladies was diagnosed, treated, and is now undergoing rehabilitation.

The resolve and strength she has shown through this process has been inspiring and she is an amazing role model not just for young girls in football but for cancer sufferers and people supporting cancer sufferers everywhere.

Hopefully the royalties from this book will go a small way towards helping the charity to continue researching and supporting families going through their own individual battles.

Andy

50 More Goalkeeper Training Exercises

Goalkeeping Practices For Soccer Coaching At Any Level

Andy Elleray

Oakamoor
Publishing

Published by Oakamoor Publishing, an imprint of Bennion Kearny Limited
6 Woodside
Churnet View Road
Oakamoor
Staffordshire
ST10 3AE

www.BennionKearny.com

Table of Contents

Introduction

Nearly five years on from my first book, the position of the goalkeeper has continued to grow into a fundamentally important position within a football team. There are more young players taking up the position than ever before, more 'goalkeeping schools' than ever before, and much more match analysis on television than ever before.

The general consensus throughout the football world is that the goalkeeper is now seen as the 11th player and not just an isolated position.

The overall aim of the book is to supply the coach or the player with a selection of practices and exercises they can use at any time. The exercises can be browsed through when designing sessions, or even deployed straight onto the training pitch.

I must stress, at this point, that the aim of these practices is not to tell you 'how' to develop the goalkeepers you're working with. Every club whether it is professional or amateur, youth academy or grassroots, England or Spain, approaches the position differently; ultimately, the book provides an opportunity to share practices that have been used at all levels of the sport in order for goalkeepers to develop the tools required to excel.

Each club/environment will have their own philosophy and fundamental ways of working whilst developing goalkeepers. The practices in this book will set the environment to work on different goalkeeping attributes whilst providing suggestions on areas that can be focussed upon within each practice.

The practices can be adapted as the reader sees fit in terms of dimensions, ball positioning, and the number of players/servers. Within the practices there will be a few key elements that look to build some realistic scenarios and situations where possible – these are as follows:

- Using a moving ball for shot-stopping practices.
- Varied shot positioning to create different angles and problems to solve – this includes working both sides of the goal when the diagram shows a specific side.

- If a ball is secured, having distribution option for the GK (sometimes mentioned in the practice descriptions).
- Rebounders to act as strikers to pounce upon loose balls.
- Vision blockers (human or mannequin) to create a sense of a crowded penalty box or situations where players are looking to close down the ball.
- Usually, one GK is shown in some practices – there can be two rotating for example.
- GKs are used as servers in the practices to work on distribution, passing range and general footwork (including 1st touch).
- Using the coach as an extra server.
- Servers/strikers in practices can take more than one role (shown with two separate numbers).

Here are practice factors that, as a coach, you should consider when conducting practices or designing a training session:

- The age and development status of each *individual* GK.
- The angles, distances and dimensions of the practices – what is relevant for your GKs?
- The repetitions and sets within each practice – again, think about what is appropriate for the environment. Within this, factor in rest rimes at RPE (Rate of Perceived Exertion) – exercise intensity level analysis.
- Coach observation – where possible, be in a position to analyse the GKs rather than being directly involved in the session (not always possible of course); think about using video analysis – see my first book *Scientific Approaches to Goalkeeping in Football* for more details.
- As a coach, look at the space and facilities available to you – the practices can be adapted at your discretion based on these factors. Also, consider the equipment shown – some pieces of equipment are not always available; for example, use cones/poles when mini goals aren't available.
- Plan where these practices fit into a training session – are they more appropriate as a warm up/introduction session or used as a main practice to relay key coaching points? With all these practices, think about appropriate warm ups (stretching, activation exercises and movement work) that will lead into the session. For example, if using a crossing practice, build plyometrics and

proprioception exercises in; or if the session is predominately based around 1v1 technical responses then lower limb flexibility and core stability exercises would serve this purpose.

This book looks to build upon the characteristics from my first title in terms of how important a holistically developed goalkeeper is. A variety of areas will be touched upon, some linking within the same practice.

Glossary

There are parts, in the supporting text, that include specific terminology that is used within the goalkeeping fraternity (of course, some coaches use variations on them as well).

For some of these, my previous books go into the specifics of the learning detail around the physical, psychological, and technical side of things – but for the purpose of this book, a short glossary is offered here.

Desire to keep the ball out of the goal: Linked to the psychological learning detail – what is the GK's attitude in challenging situations? Do they go for every ball in a practice? Do they show positive body language if goals are scored or mistakes made? Build this into a winning mentality but be careful of over-arousal – make sure the GKs show emotional control, so they don't get too pumped up if they make some great saves or get too down after a spell of goals conceded or errors. Mistakes are learning opportunities.

Being effective as an individual GK: Every GK in the world is different. Many of the basics and core attributes remain the same, however. What these practices allow is plenty of work within different scenarios but they are designed so that GKs can work to their individual styles and technical identities. GKs have different personalities, physical makeups, and ways of processing information – so bear this in mind. One size doesn't fit all.

Passing playability: Is the pass (or any distribution really) appropriate to that situation? This would include – can the receiving player control the ball easily? Is it to the correct side of their body? Will retaining the ball allow them to play forwards quickly? Where is the pressure from the opposition in relation to the intended receiver? Is the technical choice from the GK appropriate (for example, does the GK drive the ball with pace at the receiving player rather than clipping the ball for them to control easily)?

Recovery position: With a number of practices involving multiple servers – the recovery position relates to the positioning of the GKs after an initial save. Do they move back to the goal into an appropriate place to defend the goal and affect the second ball with an action? The location of the ball here is crucial to the goalkeeper's recovery position.

Hand position on the travel: If a GK is moving over a shorter distance, their hands need to be in a higher position – if the GK needs to move a shorter distance more often than not, they will be in direct threat from an attempt on goal, so hands need to be ready (nearer a set position shape). If they're travelling over a longer distance, then the ball may not be in direct threat to them, and they will need to generate momentum to move using their arms. The main point here is decelerating at the right time *with hands in the GK's specifically comfortable position* to make a save or engage a cross, etc.

Parry and deflection points: Where is the best possible place for the GK to manoeuvre the ball if they can't secure or catch it? The usual place is wide of the goal and away from immediate danger; this is good as rebounds aren't an immediate threat. However, parry or deflection points require some thinking – what's the pace on the ball? Where is the attempt coming from? Are there any other opposition players in the direct vicinity of the situation? Where are the GK's defenders? The GK won't be able to assess all of these at one time, but through coaching recall and analysis, this can be trained and reviewed (video analysis is great for these situations, to break the picture down).

Big body shape: It might be a simplistic term but it's great for younger or novice GKs. It's all about staying as big as possible (more for 1v1s) and being able to move one's limbs if necessary. Younger or novice GKs tend to go to ground easily, or be off balance, which makes it easier for the attacking player to shoot past them.

Top hand vs bottom hand assessment: Does the GK use their top or bottom hand when making a save? The train of thought is that the top hand should stay in the air longer when attempting to save high balls above the head. As a coach, analyze whether the GK has made the correct choice in how to make the save.

Timing of jump mechanics and footwork patterns: This is related to the physical but also technical learning detail, and concerns the ability of the GK to stay in control of their bodies whilst in motion. It is a crucial but hard skill to master. Areas such as stride patterns, which leg to jump/dive off, how the GK times their actions in relation to the ball (are they in sync and rhythm?) and can they accelerate/decelerate in a fast but controlled manner, all apply.

Diving fluency: This is something that takes times to develop and is related to strength, power and general coordination. Can the GK generate power to cover areas of the goal from a standing start when there is very little time (due to pace on the ball or close in position), moving their feet before a dive? When the GK is performing a diving action, be mindful of their centre of mass and if this is going directly towards the ball – whether a low, medium or high dive. The key is getting momentum *through* the ball to increase dive coverage.

Dive return: This is a term that is used in different contexts. For many (me included) this means the following: what does the GK do once they've performed a diving action, do they:

a) move directly towards the ball to engage for a second contact
b) return to their feet as quickly as possible to set where they are to make a second save
c) recover to defend the goal – this is if the ball stays, for example, in the area and there is a threat of another attempt on goal
d) recover to the goal to organise and instruct the team – for example, if the ball is saved from a diving action around the post, can the GK get to their feet as soon as possible to start this set play phase.

Re-positioning: The ability of the GK to re-position after a movement of the ball in any direction, mainly to defend the goal effectively in relation to the ball. Factors can include whether there pressure on or off the ball, where the ball has been played to, and where there is first contact – a major factor involving cutbacks and crosses.

Cross-over step vs sidestep? When the GK is travelling, do they need to cross their legs to increase their stride pattern or not? The sidestep is usually used when moving a short distance (but feet must stay close to the ground as the GK may need to stop quickly). The danger in using the wrong step method is that if the cross-over is used and the ball is struck towards the GK, they are not in a position to stop and generate movement. Vice-versa, if the GK needs to cover a longer distance and they choose to sidestep more often than not, this is slower. Stepping is affected by the GK's height, coordination, balance and ability to generate velocity.

Scanning and assessing the situation: This revolves around evaluating the individual picture a goalkeeper sees and how they best respond to the triggers they're faced with. A few examples would be – can I engage the ball? Do I need to stay and protect the goal? Do the mannequins (defenders/attackers) change my position in the goal? What is the best way to travel around the goal mouth in this situation? How am I going to save this particular ball?

1

Goalkeeping Themes: Handling and footwork.

Practice Objectives: To incorporate different handling techniques into a multi-functional and multi-directional warm up.

Description: GKs working in a small grid (dimensions can vary but as GKs get more activated this can increase). Servers deliver the ball into the grid working on selected catching techniques. Servers move to change angles/distances and receive the ball back from the GK. GK calls for the ball.

Diagram:

Progressions:

Work on one step dives, passing, volleys back, loose balls (get on the ball as quickly as possible) and high balls to work on jump mechanics.

GKs work for a pre-determined period of time.

Learning Detail:

Technical: Appropriate hand shape to the ball that's served at the GK | Set position before the ball is served to the GK | Emphasis on technical consistency | General distribution back to server

Tactical: Possible passing element and support position if the grid is made bigger

Psychological: Concentration when receiving each individual ball | Awareness of space and possible vision blocking | Communication/Information element if the GK dictates where they want the ball

Physical: Balanced movement – hands close to body if moving short distances | Ability to change direction quickly and in relation to a moving ball | General co-ordination when moving to respond to the next ball to be dealt with

Social/Environmental: For younger GKs use this as an ice-breaker | Emphasise tempo and intensity of actions

2

Goalkeeping Themes: Set Position and selection of saving techniques.

Practice Objectives: To provide the goalkeeper with a couple of varying scenarios to test their ability to set effectively, to choose which saving technique to use, and how they can be in control of their bodies whilst performing different actions.

Description: Ball starts from server 1 who drives a moving ball at the GK. They claim this ball and drop and drive the ball towards server 2 to catch (this can also be a pass to feet). Server 2 then volleys the ball back towards goal, looking to score. If the ball is caught the GK performs a throw to server 1. If parried out they look to get on the loose ball (if appropriate). They finish with a touch from server 3 around the mannequin for a strike on goal.

Each ball must be taken on its own merit and dealt with before moving on.

Diagram:

Progressions:

Change angles and distances of strikes on goal and/or distribution methods.

Learning Detail:

Technical: Consistency of handling | Timing of when, where, and how to be in set position | Detail of distribution (depending on what type worked on)

Tactical: Potential work on support position for the distribution element | Positioning off the attempt on goal from server 3 | Server 3 can also be a 1v1 save with the server advancing towards goal

Psychological: Saving decision | Recognition of trigger to drop or advance towards the ball | Focus on each individual element of the practice | Desire to keep the ball out of the goal from server 3 – being effective as an individual GK

Physical: Speed and appropriateness of footwork patterns | Balance and co-ordination during travel across the goal mouth

Social/Environmental: With other GKs doing the serving, maintain high standards and consistency of service throughout the practice

3

Goalkeeping Themes: Passing range and general shot-stopping.

Practice Objectives: To build passing practice with shot-stopping into a situation that requires quick assessments of both moving ball and players.

Description: The ball starts with server 1 acting as a centre back; they play the ball to the GK who supports the ball (near, central, or far depending on the situation), taking a touch to play to server 2. This server can change position so passing weight etc. needs to adapt. The aim is to play to the hands of server 2 who rolls the ball towards server 3; this server then attempts to score against the GK. This part can be adapted for one touch/two touch finishes or 1v1s. If the GK claims this ball, they distribute the ball to 1 or 2.

Diagram:

Progressions:

Change passing angle or distance from server 1.

Opposed distribution – support position depending on pressure and ball position.

Have server 2 rolling the ball with purpose to replicate playing into a central midfield player.

Add in mannequins for the shot-stopping part.

Learning Detail:

Technical: Consistency of handling | Timing of when, where and how to be in set position | Detail of distribution (depending on what type worked on)

Tactical: Support position for the distribution element (opposed and unopposed) | Positioning off the attempt on goal from server 3 |

Psychological: Tempo of distribution – with addition on selecting the most appropriate method based upon the target player | Assessing the direction of the ball from server 2 to 3 to decide on initial positioning | Bravery to try different passing ranges in the environment

Physical: Open body shape to receive and form stable base to play longer range passes after initial touch | Speed to cover the space in between server 3 if necessary | Showing agility to change direction with the ball and/or make big saves

Social/Environmental: With other GKs doing the serving, maintain high standards and consistency of service throughout the practice

4

Goalkeeping Themes: Passing range and general shot-stopping.

Practice Objectives: To build passing practice with shot-stopping into a situation that requires quick assessments of both moving ball and players.

Description: Ball starts with server 1 who takes a touch to shoot (mannequin can be added). If the GK secures the ball they distribute to server 2. This can be any method, however think about where the ball is secured (might be after a second save). Drop and drive could be used to practice this skill, however in a match situation it is not likely to be used with bodies in the area. If ball goes in the goal or gets saved around the post, etc – then server 2 will just get a ball. Server 2 then passes into the shaded zone for either server 1 or another player to touch and shoot on goal. If GK secures this they play to server 2.

Diagram:

Progressions:

Change server 1's shooting option (from both angle and central).

Adjust the distance and position of server 2 to be a moving target to work on pass detail.

Learning Detail:

Technical: Goal protection from server 1 – the set position is key if the ball is struck hard (no time to move feet towards the ball) | Passing accuracy to server 2 (and pass detail if a coaching focus) | Depth of positioning for the second attempt on goal

Tactical: Recovery save decision – mark a box where the GK must pounce on the bounce if not secured to avoid running after a ball that's an unrealistic distance away

Psychological: Tempo of distribution – with the addition of selecting the most appropriate method based upon the target player | Saving decision from servers 1 and 3 | Determination to be consistent in all actions | Emotional control – if a great save from server 1, keep level head throughout

Physical: Ability to produce power to dive through the ball from server 1 | Keep shape and kicking base when playing to server 2 | Early and fast footwork to travel towards the ball for server 3 | Dive return (back on feet to save/recovery save) after initial save from attempt on goal

Social/Environmental: With other GKs doing the serving, maintain high standards and consistency of service throughout the practice

5

Goalkeeping Themes: Technical selection based upon ball positioning.

Practice Objectives: To expose the GKs to situations where they must decide when, where, and how to travel then position for a through ball/slid ball. Is this situation a traditional 1v1 or shot-stopping picture?

Description: The ball starts with server 1 anywhere in the shaded zone. They touch and play down the side of the mannequins for either server 1 or 3 for an attempt on goal. The weight and direction of this pass will change for each repetition giving the GK a new problem to solve each time. If the GK secures the ball, build in a distribution zone/goal or play back to a player.

Diagram:

Progressions:

Change passing and shooting angles/distances.

The opposite server can act as a rebounder for balls parried out towards the mannequins.

Learning Detail:

Technical: Shot-stopping technique (catch, parry, deflect, kick through) or 1v1 (smother, block, repel) in relation to the situation | Ability to guide the ball away from goal if the ball can't be secured at first

Tactical: Initial depth/width of start position in relation to the ball | Positioning upon point of contact

Psychological: Early assessment of picture (1v1 or shot on goal from further distance) | Choice and execution of action | Focus on the triggers to drop or advance based upon strikers touch and/or ball positioning

Physical: Initial speed to cover distance and engage the ball played by server 1 if necessary | Ability to decelerate and set in rhythm with the play in front of them | General reactive agility to produce movements to cover the goal as best as possible given the situation

Social/Environmental: With other GKs doing the serving, maintain high standards and consistency of service throughout the practice | Emphasis on match tempo in this zone – in a match these combinations are very quick and decisive

6

Goalkeeping Themes: Central entries (with blocked vision shooting).

Practice Objectives: To expose the GK to a situation that involves quick passing around the box and attempts on goal with players/mannequins in the eye-line of the GK. Focus would be on depth in the goal mouth.

Description: The ball starts with server 1 who plays to GK who then recycles the ball to server 2. This server plays the ball to a player situated just outside the area (this can be altered). This server will either take a touch and shoot or shoot first time through the mannequin alignment. It's important the player who shoots takes different types of touches to change the GK's thought process.

Diagram:

Progressions:

Change the angle and distances of servers 1 and 2.

Add in a rebounder for a potential second attempt on goal.

Learning Detail:

Technical: First touch to play in the direction of server 2 | Passing playability to server 2 | Goal protection decision based upon ball positioning, flight and direction

Tactical: Initial depth/width of start position in relation to the ball | Positioning upon point of contact of the attempt on goal

Psychological: Assessment of touch/movement of the shooting server | Focus on the path of the ball through the mannequins | Ability to change decision on technique used, based upon deflections or change of direction of the ball

Physical: Speed of footwork and body shape to pass out | Getting the body through the ball when diving – if there's no time to move feet laterally to dive, the set position is crucial | Agility and co-ordination to change direction as quickly as possible to defend the goal

Social/Environmental: With other GKs doing the serving, maintain high standards and consistency of service throughout the practice | Emphasis on match tempo in this zone – in a match these combinations are very quick and decisive

7

Goalkeeping Themes: Cutbacks (with blocked vision shooting).

Practice Objectives: To enhance understanding of positioning from cutbacks and the execution of different techniques (where, when, and how); the shaded zone is the area worked for attempts on goal.

Description: The ball starts centrally from server 1; they touch out of feet and play to server 2 who either plays first or second time. The direction of their cutback can be between mannequins for a first time finish from server 3 or a cutback to the edge of the box for a first or second time finish from this server. Rebounds and recovery saves/lines are in place. Add a distribution zone if possible as well.

Diagram:

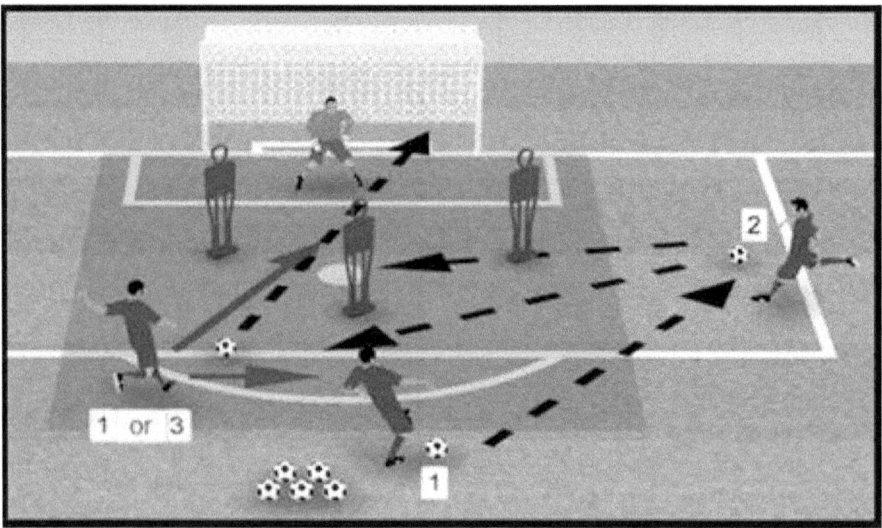

Progressions:

Change the positioning of server 2.

Add in a time limit to finish (rather than touches) but the emphasis must be on a fast tempo.

Learning Detail:

Technical: Efficiency of footwork to get in the most effective position as early as possible | Focus on the choice of technique but most importantly the speed in which the technique is chosen

Tactical: Position from initial cutback – follow the ball but don't over-compensate at the front post | If pressure on the ball (replicated by mannequins) think about dropping to increase reaction time

Psychological: Early assessment of picture (1v1 or shot on goal from further distance) | Choice and execution of action | Ability to perform consistently in choice of position and how the ball is looked to be saved

Physical: Initial speed to cover distance and engage the ball played by server 1 if necessary (when the ball is played across the face of goal) | Speed of body and limbs to protect the goal as best as possible | Pattern of travel movement across the goal mouth (balance/co-ordination)

Social/Environmental: Make sure the focus is on the GK and the others learning from the detailed coaching points and not on the players scoring goals

8

Goalkeeping Themes: Cutback scenarios with reaction saves.

Practice Objectives: To provide the GK with scenarios where they have to assess the ball played across the goal – the idea is to provide them with three main decisions – do I hold back and set? Can I engage the ball? Do I hold and intercept the ball before it's played past me?

Description: The ball starts with server 1 who touches the ball out of feet and looks to play across the GK. There can be a mannequin to act as a closing down defender. The scenario plays out with the three main decisions as stated above – server 2 can be on different conditions such as – first touch finish, touch and finish, or advance to goal. In this zone, the finishes are usually first time so bear this in mind.

Diagram:

Progressions:

Add mannequins in different positions in the penalty box to represent different areas of pressure on the ball; this will affect the GK's decision where to position themselves.

Put in a distribution zone if the ball is secured – possibly counter attack due to the scenario.

Learning Detail:

Technical: Technical decisions analysis – interception of cutback technique (low dive or guide the ball away?) | Engagement in 1v1 technique (blocks or smothers?) | Shot-stopping reaction technique (one step dive, kick through for low shots or repel save?)

Tactical: Position from initial cutback – follow ball but don't over-compensate at the front post | If pressure on the ball (replicated by mannequins) think about dropping to increase reaction time | Recovery save or recovery line position after a first save

Psychological: Early assessment of picture based on the cutback (the three main decisions as stated above) | Choice and execution of action | Ability to perform consistently in choice of position and how the ball is looked to be saved | Not be discouraged if goals are being scored

Physical: Initial speed to cover distance and engage the ball played by server 1 if necessary (when the ball is played across the face of goal) | Speed of body and limbs to protect the goal as best as possible | Pattern of travel movement across the goal mouth (balance/co-ordination)

Social/Environmental: Make sure focus is on the GK and the others learning from the detailed coaching points and not on the players scoring goals | Show bravery in all situations and look to set an example in the goalkeeping group

9

Goalkeeping Themes: Crossing into specific zone (with shot-stopping element).

Practice Objectives: To provide the GK with crossed ball situations – with the coach possibly focusing on one kind of delivery area with the GK. There is a specific zone for a target delivery. Think about if you actually need this as the GK may pre-empt their movements if they know the potential target zone.

Description: The ball will start from server 1 with them delivering a cross – this could be stationary or touch to cross (depending on the player). The GK will deal with the ball however they see appropriate. If they secure the ball, they can play into server 2 who will play the ball back to the central server for a strike on goal. If server 1's ball is punched or goes over the bar, for example, then server 2 will play a ball into the central player.

Diagram:

Progressions:

Place an emphasis on the distribution element by moving the target player to a full back position, for example, and work on this detail.

Require a longer pass for a counter attack based upon the crossing scenario.

Learning Detail:

Technical: How the GK deals with the crossed ball (catch, punch etc.) | Quality, appropriateness and consistency of distribution | Technical selection based upon attempt on the goal

Tactical: Initial position from the crossing position (higher or deeper depending on your GK) | Distribution selection and detail based upon the receiving player's position

Psychological: Early assessment of the crossed ball | Confidence to come into a crowded area | Awareness of the positioning of the striker and their touch/decision with the ball

Physical: Footwork relating to the cross (shoulder and hip rotations) | Jumping mechanics and timing of movements | Travel pattern from squared pass (hands close if ball travels a short distance so GK is ready for attempt on goal | Diving mechanics in relation to the height of ball

Social/Environmental: Match tempo and intent with distribution elements

10

Goalkeeping Themes: Blocking techniques.

Practice Objectives: To allow the GK to be introduced and be comfortable with making blocking saves from close range. The emphasis will be on making these after an initial diving save to replicate a parry.

Description: The ball starts from server 1 who puts the GK into a low diving save (the practice will work both sides). The ball will be returned to server 1 while the GK is on the ground. The GK will then get off the ground towards server 2's ball and perform a blocking save. Server 2 will time their movement in accordance with the GK returning to his or her feet and will get the first contact.

Diagram:

Progressions:

Potential second save from the same side as the blocking was performed on.

Play live off the block for a recovery save after engagement.

Change the ball position for a blocked save (further away or at a different angle for each repetition or each set).

Learning Detail:

Technical: Head position for a block needs to be towards the ball | Stride pattern to engage ball needs to allow for explosive movement | Arms spread and forwards | Legs split and low to ground to avoid nutmeg

Tactical: If using two saves, recovery position if the ball is too far away or not appropriate to engage

Psychological: Willingness to put body into this position | Speed of assessment of ball position | Confidence to try new techniques in the environment | Patience in obtaining the optimum timing within the practice as it will take time to develop

Physical: Speed with balance towards the ball | Strong core and tensing of body to obtain optimum blocking position | Co-ordination of body shape with timing upon the initial contact from server | Flexibility in lower limbs to create spreading position and angles

Social/Environmental: Use softer balls at first, if necessary, to reduce impact on the body and for novice players to increase bravery and timing of movement patterns

11

Goalkeeping Themes: Recovery save scenario (with focus on dive return).

Practice Objectives: To provide the GK with opportunities to work on recovery saves with different points of ball entry into the goal area.

Description: The ball will start from server 1 who will put the GK into a mid or low diving save facing away from the post. The GK will throw the ball to server 2 from the ground to catch above their eye-line. The GK will then return to their feet and travel in response to the ball from server 3 who will take a touch to strike. If the GK secures the ball, there is a distribution goal or target zone.

Diagram:

Progressions:

Have the main attempt on goal coming from another ball from server 1 (or another player around the playing area).

Server 2 can potentially give the working GK another save of some description (1v1, loose ball, hard volley or standard strike on goal).

Learning Detail:

Technical: Forward dive angle and step through the ball from server 1 | Hand position on the travel from server 1 to 3 | Technical choice on save from server 3 | Ability to clear the penalty box with deflection or parry hand position

Tactical: General positioning from the servers (depth, width, movement with the ball, into or down the line | Focus on getting into line first rather than down the line (cover goal first and can adjust after)

Psychological: Awareness and assessment of server 3's position (if this changes for every attempt on goal, the GK will have to adapt and not get into a mental rhythm) | Decision on goal protection technique from server 3 and or 2 if working on two saves

Physical: Goal coverage from server 3 | Hands vs no hands to return to feet | Speed and balance on the travel to server 3 | Set position ready for potential no step dive if the ball is struck hard | Efficiency of footwork patterns through the practice

Social/Environmental: Make sure the focus is on the GK and the others learning from detailed coaching points and not on the players scoring goals

12

Goalkeeping Themes: Angled shot-stopping (basic level practice).

Practice Objectives: To give the GK an opportunity to work on angled shot-stopping in this final phase of an attack.

Description: The ball is with the single server who touches either side and at any distance past the mannequin for a strike on goal. The server will look to score anywhere in the goal with different ball contacts such as side foot, driven, curling or toe poke.

Diagram:

Progressions:

Add in a distribution option if the ball is secured and practice any given method (possibly one the GK needs to work on).

Learning Detail:

Technical: Forward dive angle on saves – mark out some cones (indicated by the lines behind the GK in the diagram) to encourage this and spot for this action | Parry and deflection points – strong wrists and ability to manoeuvre the ball away from the goal

Tactical: General positioning from the initial touch (look at how far the GK moves laterally and down the line) | If a distribution element is added then focus on the detail behind a receiving player on the method selected

Psychological: Save selection and speed/appropriateness of this selection | Respond to different types of strikes (as mentioned in the description) as this could alter the GK's decision

Physical: Balanced set position after the initial touch from the server | Reactive agility focus as the GK will not know where the ball is going | Flexibility in the lower legs if kick through or leg-based saves are used (if you worked on these)

Social/Environmental: Make sure the focus is on the GK and the others learning from the detailed coaching points and not on the players scoring goals

13

Goalkeeping Themes: Red Zone Entries – different goal protection scenarios.

Practice Objectives: To give the GK exposure to a variety of different shot-stopping angles and distances. The Red Zone is split into 1-7 yards, 7-14 yards, and 14-21 yards, to indicate different ranges of attempts on goal, which will require the GK to select different techniques to keep the ball out of the goal.

Description: Servers are placed outside the Red Zone will a ball each (three shown in this practice). These servers are moving around manipulating the ball. Upon the coach's call, one server will advance into any part of the zone and attempt to score. The process will then begin again. If the GK secures the ball they distribute it back to that server; if the ball is parried back into the Red Zone then all the servers can have a maximum two touch rebound attempt. There can be mannequins in the practice too.

Diagram:

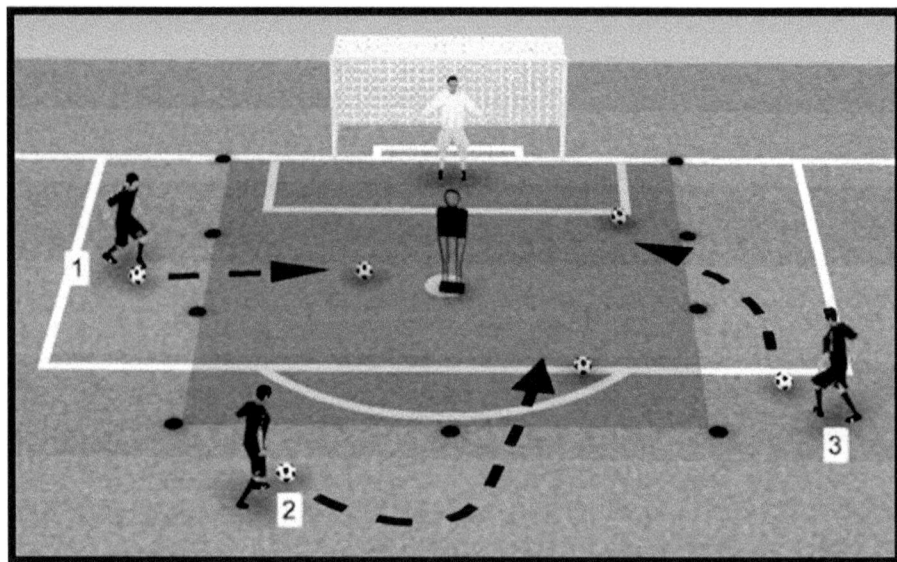

Progressions:

No call for the server from the coach; there is communication between the servers as to who attacks.

Rotate the GKs – have a competition; you stay in goal until you concede.

Learning Detail:

Technical: Save selection is based upon the distance or specific area of the Red Zone the attempt is taken from; 1-7 yards = 1v1, for example | Set position upon point of contact for the attempt

Tactical: Movement into position to affect advancing server | Initial starting position in the goal area

Psychological: Decision when to engage the ball | Concentration within the practice as servers' attempts will be intermittent | Ability to choose the most appropriate technique given the position of the attempt on goal

Physical: Speed of movement to the server who is attacking | General agility and flexibility in making saves and physically responding to the scenario | The timing of the set position within the Red Zone

Social/Environmental: Make sure focus is on the GK and the others learning from the detailed coaching points and not on the players scoring goals

14

Goalkeeping Themes: Shot-stopping with an initial movement.

Practice Objectives: To test the GK's set position after some initial movements. This practice can involve a single server or a second save/action to add a different element to the practice.

Description: The GK faces server 1 who calls 'pole or post'; the GK will touch either of these and return to the line of the ball for a strike on ball (touch and strike with either foot from server 1). The second action from server 2 (optional) can either be a distribution method to a target zone/player, or a loose ball where the GK has to pounce on the ball.

Diagram:

Progressions:

Change angle and distance of server 1's attempt on goal.

Server 2 can be a 1v1 scenario where the GK must advance past the pole to make a save.

Learning Detail:

Technical: General shot-stopping principles – think about dive angle going forwards of the pole | Any distribution method if the ball is secured | If using a 1v1 for server 2, focus on angle approach to the ball

Tactical: Movement into position to affect advancing server | Initial starting position in the goal area

Psychological: Speed of decision to touch the pole or post | Assessment of the ball and the speed of response

Physical: Focus on the GK's dive coverage and the height they're diving in relation to the height of the ball | If using a short distance for the attempt on goal – work on how, and when, to use the legs to make saves

Social/Environmental: Make the attempts on goal challenging and at match tempo and intensity given where the practice is geographically taking place on the pitch

15

Goalkeeping Themes: Reaction and blocking saves (Emergency Goal Protection).

Practice Objectives: To test the GK's reactions and their ability to put their body on the line to make last ditch match-winning saves.

Description: The ball starts from server 1 who has the option of striking from a position right next to the ball or playing to server 2 who has a first time strike to score. Make the GK aware that the odds are massively in favour of the servers to score to set realistic expectations here. Soft balls can be used for this practice, as well, to build confidence and avoid repetitive impacts.

Diagram:

Progressions:

Work both sides of the goal.

Change the position of the ball with subtle changes such as server 2 moving closer or further away from the goal – but keep the emphasis on close range.

Have a ball movement to server 1 before their initial strike to start the practice.

Learning Detail:

Technical: Emphasis on speed of body and limbs towards the ball | Assess which is quicker to the ball: leg or hand? | Big body shape with focus on the head position as this will dictate balance and torso position/posture

Tactical: Movement into position from server 2 – Ball/Body/Goal

Psychological: Speed of assessment if ball is shifted to the side | Bravery and confidence to withstand impact of the ball from a close-range distance and at a possible high velocity | How the GK looks to save the ball and with which body part

Physical: Co-ordination of limbs if needing to make a reaction save from server 1 | Footwork pattern and balance if the GK needs to travel across the goal | Does the GK need to stand up and be a presence or is it a case of just diving full length in front of the ball?

Social/Environmental: Make the attempts on goal challenging and at match tempo and intensity given where the practice is geographically taking place on the pitch

16

Goalkeeping Themes: Saving techniques incorporating activation and footwork patterns.

Practice Objectives: To allow the GK to go through a range of saves in a controlled environment – ideal for a warm up or before a specific session to introduce some technical points.

Description: The GK starts on the back cone and moves in a fast but controlled manner into the coned gate. They then receive a type of service from this server (for example: 1 or 2 touch passing, scoop saves, clips or driven pass to hands). The GK can roll back, put the ball down and pass back, or place the ball to drive the ball back to the server. The GK will then move backwards to the initial cone before moving to the opposite gate. If more than 3 GKs have 2 working at a time.

Diagram:

Progressions:

Rotate GKs after a set number of repetitions.

Have different service types from servers (1 has a scoop, another has a pass). Also, build in diving saves at different heights and step ranges as the GKs become warmer.

Change angles and distances of servers' positions – make gates wider for GK to cover.

Learning Detail:

Technical: Hands close to body as travelling a short distance | Footwork patterns that allow quick movement but also maintain balance and control of body | Consistency of first touch, general handling and set position

Tactical: No real tactical element in this practice – unless you build in a longer range passing option where the GK needs to select the best option for that player

Psychological: Attention on consistency within all actions | When the service becomes less prescribed, the selection of techniques will be brought into consideration

Physical: 360 degree movements | Balance and co-ordination when moving between gates and cones | Steady upper body – head and shoulders still

Social/Environmental: Lots of emphasis on the right tempo and intensity | Energy and enthusiasm – if this is used as an initial practice, it can set the tone for the session

17

Goalkeeping Themes: Cutback situations – involving blocking and reaction saves.

Practice Objectives: To allow the GK to experiment with different start positions when facing cutback situations – from both left and right foot service. The emphasis must be on making quick decisions and an appreciation that there will be goals scored in all variations of this practice.

Description: The ball starts with server 1 who will touch out of feet to initiate the practice (left or right touch). This will be anywhere within the length of the 6 yard box and a couple of yards away (but this can vary). The ball will be played either towards server 2 or 3 for a first time finish. The pace of this pass will vary so the GK has to take this into account when deciding where and how to position themselves.

Diagram:

Progressions:

Have servers 2 and 3 running in or holding their positions.

Add mannequins for a more advanced approach.

Learning Detail:

Technical: Ability to repel the ball away from the immediate danger area for rebounds – based on players and where the save is made | Strong hands and wrists | Select the tool to use early and make this relevant to height, pace, and direction of the ball

Tactical: When, where, and how to engage the attacker taking into account the information available: pace of the ball, can I engage/intercept, do I need to cover the space to follow the ball, do I hold and set upon contact, how am I going to save the ball and with what body part?

Psychological: Motivation and desire to stop the ball going in the goal | To keep pursuing an optimum approach for the GK to achieve success relative to their stage of development and understanding | Not to dwell on goals conceded – odds are in attackers' favour

Physical: Head positioning and physical capacity to hold shape | Flexibility in lower limbs in order to move them quickly to save the ball | Speed and agility to cover the ball – last ditch dives or chase lost causes | Initial stance before the ball is cutback

Social/Environmental: Emphasise the importance of the quality of service at all times and the speed of play

18

Goalkeeping Themes: Early and quick strikes in the penalty area.

Practice Objectives: To give the GK exposure to early and quick shots with bodies and regular movements of the ball. The emphasis will be on the GK to respond to different angles of passes into servers, different types of touches (towards/away from goal or towards/away from pressure), and to different types of finishes (placed, driven, lofted and 1v1s).

Description: The ball starts with server 1 who can play in from a central position which is indicated by the line. They touch out of feet and play into servers 2 or 3 who can take a touch or shoot first time. The ball is live until secured by the GK, a goal is scored, or the ball is saved out of bounds or out the penalty area. Servers change receiving position after every repetition. Add in a distribution target as well if you feel it necessary to work on this transition with your GKs.

Diagram:

Progressions:

Have servers 2 and 3 starting in behind the mannequins.

Use real bodies instead of mannequins if you have the numbers.

Learning Detail:

Technical: Specific technical action in response to the ball | Look at the appropriateness in this action and whether it is effective or not – for example, is the GK using a 1v1 technique for a longer range attempt on goal?

Tactical: Initial positioning in relation to the ball and the initial ball movement | Down the line or hold? How wide do I need to go in the goal if the touch is wider?

Psychological: Assessment of the picture – where is the ball? Where are the mannequins? What can I do in this situation to save the ball? | Commit to the technical action fully

Physical: Balanced set position at the point of contact | Goal coverage (speed, power and co-ordination of movement) | Recovery save situations – look at how quickly the GK returns to their feet or their second action

Social/Environmental: Emphasise the importance of the quality of service at all times and the speed of play

19

Goalkeeping Themes: High aerial balls towards goal with an additional angled attempt to replicate a rebound.

Practice Objectives: To give the GK work on high aerial balls that reach them at different heights and speeds but with an emphasis on above their head. If the ball hits the bar or is rebounded out, the ball is still live or there will be a second save.

Description: The ball starts with server 1 who delivers a dipping volley over the mannequins for the GK to attempt to save. If the GK secures the ball they distribute out to server 2 who takes a touch and strikes on goal. If ball hits the bar or is pushed back into the area, both servers can come alive and look to score (have a time limit for fast play). If the ball goes over the bar or the GK deflects it over/wide, move to server 2 for a strike as they'll have a selection of balls ready.

Diagram:

Progressions:

Change the angle of the dipping volley.

Move server 2 around, add in some more mannequins or change the position of vision blockers.

Learning Detail:

Technical: Top hand vs bottom hand assessment | Ability to alter hand shape and position depending on the flight path and the pace on the ball

Tactical: Initial depth from the dipping volley – bouncing ball, mannequin placement are factors | Positioning for the rebound or second save – quick judgement upon where the ball rebounds to, and the positioning of attackers

Psychological: Concentration throughout the phase of judging the ball | Decision of actions and movement from the dipping volley | Attention on handling within the whole practice phase

Physical: Timing of jump mechanics and footwork patterns to move backwards | Drop off of shoulders depending on which side of the GK the ball goes | Ability to generate power to jump backwards and/or laterally

Social/Environmental: Service from the dipping volley can be varied so the path of the ball doesn't become predictable

20

Goalkeeping Themes: Speed and efficiency of footwork, and the speed of re-positioning, based on a travelling ball.

Practice Objectives: To expose the GK to situations where they have to adapt to a travelling ball by assessing the picture then moving in relation to the ball.

Description: The ball will start with server 1 who will bounce the ball. Upon the bounce, the GK will start to drop off back to the goal line and at this point the server will perform a dipping volley to try and score back over the GK's head. If the GK catches the ball, they roll it into a mini goal or to another server and proceed across the goal to server 3 who will have a ball. Server 3 will touch the ball forwards to shoot, or play across to server 1 for a first time finish. If the ball goes over or in the goal after the dipping volley, then the GK will go straight to server 3 as a start point. Any rebounds from this phase will see both servers 1 and 3 live on a first time finish.

Diagram:

Progressions:

Move servers 1 and 3 around the penalty box, with server 1 being able to take a touch from the cutback.

Change the distribution method or picture after the first serve to the GK.

Server 2 can have a third attempt on goal to finish with.

Learning Detail:

Technical: Handling shape from dipping volley | Technical response to the attempt on goal

Tactical: Adjustment from first action | Assess where server 3's ball is, and where best to be best positioned

Psychological: Overall speed of decision making | Positive and dominating body language

Physical: Ability to adjust to the dipping volley – head, shoulder and hip rotation of dropping off | Be wary of back-peddling as it's hard to generate upwards momentum | Set position from first time strike

Social/Environmental: Set a high paced, high tempo practice but emphasise control of body and limbs from the GKs

21

Goalkeeping Themes: Technical response within the 7-14 yard zone (as seen with shaded area) – this will test a GK's decision making ability within a key part of the penalty box.

Practice Objectives: To expose the GK to a specific focus on saves within the penalty box. The 7-14 yard zone is often an area where responses can be mixed (staying deep when the GK could have engaged the ball or coming down the line when they've got little chance of effecting the ball). This practice will look to test this.

Description: The ball will start with server 1 taking a touch out of their feet; they have four ways of entry into this zone: 1) play ball into space 2) travel in with the ball to shoot on their next touch 3) slide the ball into server 2 or 3 to shoot 4) combine with server 2 or 3. Due to the four entry ways, the GK should get a variety of situations and a different picture at each repetition.

Diagram:

Progressions:

Add in a time limit to enhance speed of play if necessary.

Build in a counter attack option to work on breaking the line and side-volleying.

Learning Detail:

Technical: Focus on the detail within the technical responses that are focused on; for example, is the GK protecting the goal or engaging the ball?

Tactical: Adjustment from first action and how the GK responds to the four ways of entry – look if the attacker has control of the ball

Psychological: Overall speed of decision making | Positive and dominating body language | Have the confidence to try new techniques and ways of being an effective GK in their own unique style

Physical: Set position and weight transference will be tested here – important for the coach to observe and not serve if possible | Speed to cover the distance in front of the GK | General agility and co-ordination when dealing with the ball – with lots of saving methods available, pin-point the ones to focus on

Social/Environmental: Focus on the quality of service; this would be a good opportunity to use outfield players if available

22

Goalkeeping Themes: 1v1 techniques – blocking, spreading, lower limb interventions and smothering.

Practice Objectives: To enhance a GK's technical ability in a variety of 1v1 technical responses. The practice design will allow for lots of repetition in a high energy environment. The main goals are 10 yards apart.

Description: The ball will start with either server who will act as attacker (server 1 in this diagram). On a verbal or visual trigger (a shout or bounce of the ball) both 1 and 2 will run around the goal and back into the playing area for the attacker to try and score with the GK closing the ball down and engaging the ball as they best see fit. Once this ball is finished, the attacking server will move into the goal, either side of theirs, for a first time strike from the coach or other server. Rotate attacking players as you see fit.

Diagram:

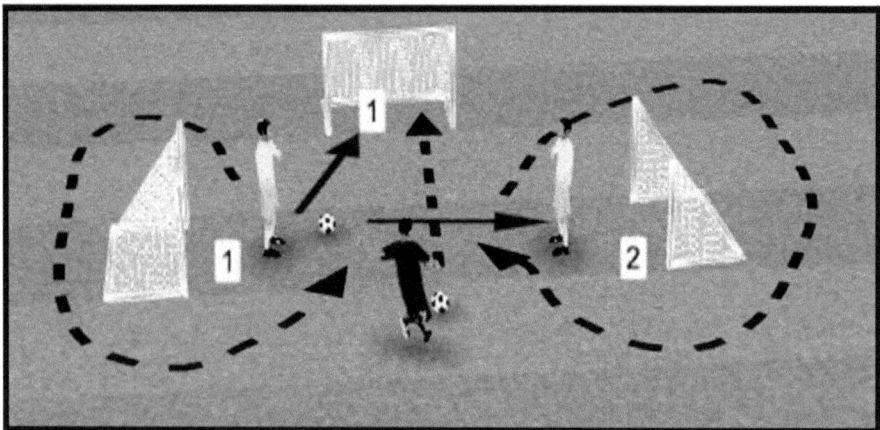

Progressions:

Change distances and angles of the ball – the coach can move the ball mid-run.

Make goals smaller and bigger (small goals shown in this diagram)

Use softer balls when necessary to build confidence in developing new techniques.

Learning Detail:

Technical: Approach to the ball and the technical proficiency and consistency of the action | Head position over the ball when possible | Avoid being a 'ramp' which sees the ball go up and over the chest

Tactical: Ball/Body/Goal – body between the ball and goal to help execute technique and display physical prowess

Psychological: Determination and decisiveness of action – don't let the ball just hit you; tense and engage the body to become a wall | Awareness of the ball position upon approaching the ball

Physical: Ability to decelerate or to carry on through the ball | Speed and co-ordination of upper and lower limbs towards the ball | General speed and agility to move around the ball

Social/Environmental: High tempo and competitive nature | Channel aggression into desire to keep the ball out of the goal

23

Goalkeeping Themes: 1v1 techniques – blocking, spreading, lower limb interventions and smothering with some distribution involved.

Practice Objectives: To explore 1v1s using different approaches and in a varied practice environment where certain constraints can be altered to change the outcomes (changing pitch and goal size, time limits and touch limits). Pitch will start with the goals 10 yards apart.

Description: The coach starts with the ball and picks a GK to start – in this diagram GK 1. The coach passes the ball in with the starting GK passing to 2, 2 passing to 3, and 3 then back to 1. Once the starting GK receives the ball, they can advance and try to score in either goal with a three second time limit. Once the ball is finished, the process starts again.

Diagram:

Progressions:

Different distribution methods between GKs.

Coach changes entry point of the ball – and can have an attempt on any goal for a second save for GKs; this can take the form of the server entering the playing area to try and score.

Ball can be played around continuously – when coach shouts 'GO', the GK in possession will attack.

Learning Detail:

Technical: Approach to the ball, alongside technical proficiency and consistency of the action | Head position over the ball when possible | Avoid being a 'ramp' where the ball goes up and over the chest | Consistency of kicking and throwing skills when playing between GKs

Tactical: Ball/Body/Goal – body between the ball and goal to help execute technique and display physical prowess

Psychological: Determination and decisiveness of action – don't let the ball just hit you; tense and engage the body to become a wall | Awareness of the ball position once approaching the ball

Physical: Ability to decelerate or to carry on through the ball | Speed and co-ordination of upper and lower limbs towards the ball | General speed and agility to move around the ball

Social/Environmental: High tempo and competitive nature | Channel aggression into desire to keep the ball out of the goal

24

Goalkeeping Themes: 1v1 techniques – blocking, spreading, lower limb interventions and smothering with some distribution involved.

Practice Objectives: To explore 1v1s in a couple of different settings, with different striking points at different angles. The playing area can vary in size – but bear in mind the theme of the practices are utilising 1v1 techniques and close ball engagement.

Description: In the diagram, on the left, the ball starts with server 1 who plays into server 2 for a first time strike at either goal. GKs will start on the near post and follow the path of the ball. The diagram on the right is a suggested progression which involves more GKs and different serving points. There can be two entry points for the ball (server 1 and 2) or just start with 1. In this example, the ball will be played from alternative sides and ball is in play until it's in a goal or outside the playing area. GKs can strike at other goals if the ball is loose in the playing area.

Diagram:

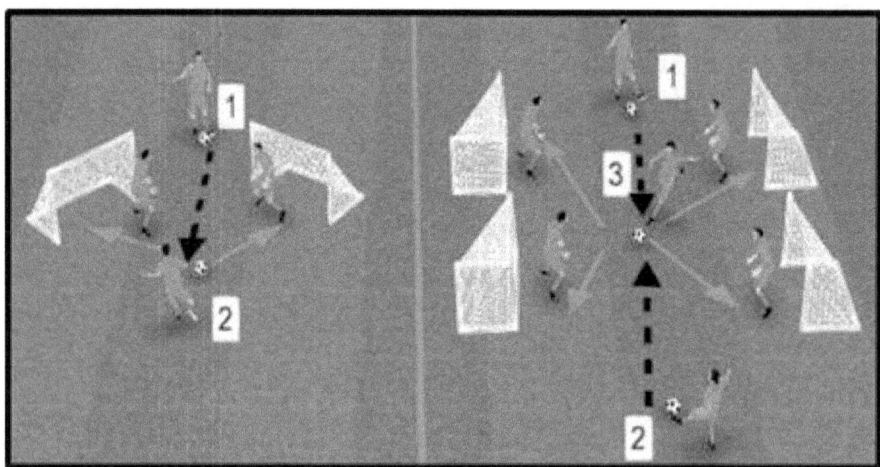

Progressions:

Different entry point angles for the ball.

Rotate GKs and servers in each practice.

Learning Detail:

Technical: Ability to hold shape and recover from the ground quickly | Responses appropriate to the height, speed and direction of the ball

Tactical: Ball/Body/Goal – body between the ball and goal to help execute technique and display physical prowess

Psychological: Determination and decisiveness of action – don't let the ball just hit the GK; tense and engage the body to become a wall | Concentration and focus on the ball that's in play and the response time to shift position and travel the distance to the ball

Physical: Ability to decelerate or to carry on through the ball | Speed and co-ordination of upper and lower limbs towards the ball | General speed and agility to move around the ball

Social/Environmental: High tempo and competitive nature | Channel aggression into desire to keep the ball out of the goal

25

Goalkeeping Themes: Rebounds and recovery saves.

Practice Objectives: To allow the GK to work on rebounds and different types of recovery saves.

Description: The ball starts with server 1 who will provoke a diving save from hands or feet (various heights depending on GK's individual focus or rotation of methods). If the GK parries or pushes the ball away, server 2 will act as the rebound from this ball. If the GK catches the ball, they throw the ball whilst on the ground towards the cone and return to feet and receive a first time attempt on goal from server 2 aiming anywhere on the goal. If the ball is still not dealt with, server 1 can have an additional rebound. For a conditioning element, have the GK diving on the first ball they have to deal with – similar to a loose ball.

Diagram:

Progressions:

Different angles and position of server 2's strike (see ball dispersal).

Service from server 1 (type and position of serve)

Learning Detail:

Technical: Upper body still whilst travelling | Handling decision based upon factors such as distance of strike, pace, and trajectory of the ball | Ability to guide or force the ball into a 'safe' area away from the immediate goal mouth/penalty box

Tactical: Recovery position after initial diving action | Assess the possibility of engaging the first ball if not secured

Psychological: Be composed and in control of actions | Concentration all the way until the ball is dealt with | Speed of decision and readiness from the rebound (as this will be an instantaneous strike)

Physical: Initial diving angle and coverage (emphasise diving through the ball) | Observe how the GK gets off the floor – with/without hands, initial steps, and the timing of when they're set

Social/Environmental: Emphasise consistency and the ethos of everyone challenging each other

26

Goalkeeping Themes: General handling with movement and co-ordination patterns.

Practice Objectives: To allow the GK to work on some basic foundations including set position timing/stance, basic handling shapes, relevant footwork patterns, and ball familiarity. The square the GK operates in will be 6x6 yards.

Description: The GK starts facing server 1 and they'll receive a strike in and around them (the type at the coach's discretion). They will then drop and drive the ball back to this server before moving to face server 2 for a 1-2 short pass (in-line with the cones). After this action, the GK will drop off to receive a volley serve from server 3 – this volley can be a side-winder, dipping volley, half volley or full volley.

Diagram:

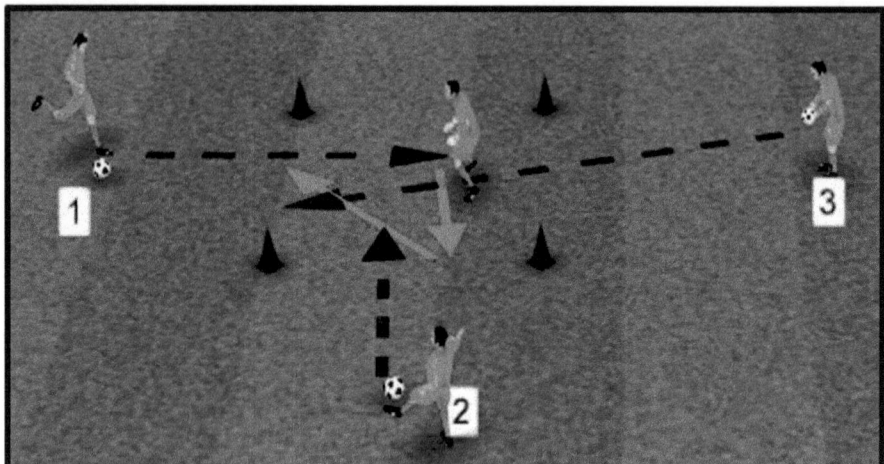

Progressions:

Different types of service throughout – loose balls, aerial balls, or diving actions.

Change the size of the box GK operates in, and the distances of servers.

Learning Detail:

Technical: Upper body still whilst travelling | Handling decision based upon factors such as distance of strike, pace, and trajectory of the ball | Passing accuracy and weight of pass

Tactical: No real tactical element – the focus is mostly on technical repetition, and physical control

Psychological: Be composed and in control of actions | Focus on the cleanliness of handling and the efficiency of footwork

Physical: Ability to be set and balanced before each action | Observe the dropping off phase to check for appropriate stride patterns and hip/shoulder rotation | From the volley, look to be aggressive and meet the ball – not standing with weight back so the ball could ricochet off the GK

Social/Environmental: Emphasise consistency and the ethos of everyone challenging each other

27

Goalkeeping Themes: Goal mouth movements with various shot-stopping opportunities.

Practice Objectives: To expose the GK to a variety of random shot-stopping scenarios in a chaotic setting. The smaller poled goals will be four yards in width.

Description: The practice starts with server 2 playing a ball aimed at the poled goal on the right – with the GK starting behind the nearest mannequin. This GK will attempt to keep the ball out of this goal. After this, server 1 will play a pass in front of the mannequins for server 2 to have a first time strike on goal which they're looking to score from.

Diagram:

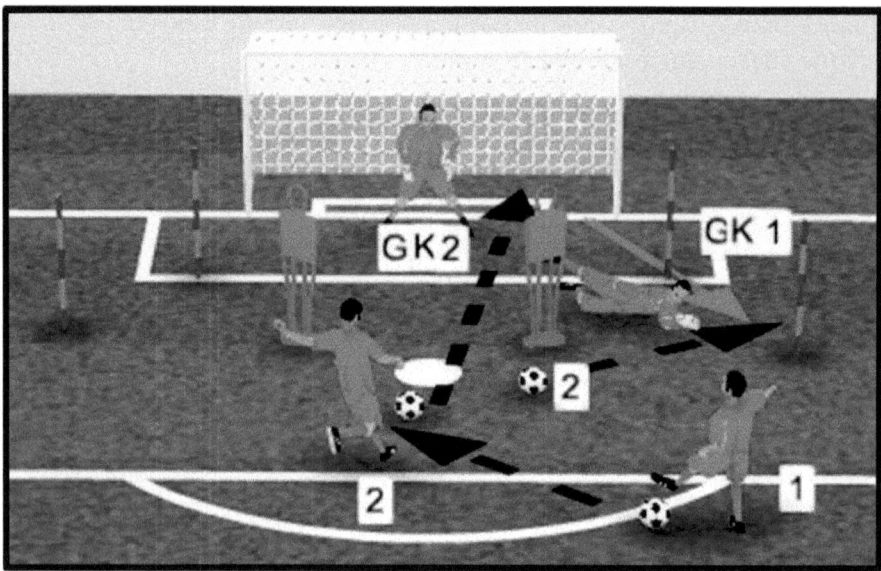

Progressions:

GK1 can receive a second save from either server to defend the same mini goal the first ball was struck towards.

Bring the whole practice in by six yards to focus on a more reactive and fast-paced practice.

Add a distribution element if the ball is secured by GK2.

Learning Detail:

Technical: GK1 leads with the hands towards the ball | GK2's technical response to the specific attempt on goal | Observe diving action – is there time to shift feet and dive? Does the GK use a negative dive? Or is the best option to set and dive?

Tactical: GK2's position in relation to the passed ball from server 1 – height, depth and lateral movement

Psychological: Awareness of the ball and not to be distracted by mannequins and the movement of players | Decision making in terms of both GKs' responses to the balls they face

Physical: Speed of travel and intent from GK1 – look out for a stride pattern that gets them as close to the ball as possible and not to dive early if unnecessary | Ability of GK2 to change position sharply off the pass | Set position upon the first contact from server 2 before their strike on goal – when to set?

Social/Environmental: Emphasise consistency and the ethos of everyone challenging each other

28

Goalkeeping Themes: Technical repetition – handling, diving and 1v1 saves.

Practice Objectives: To provide the GKs with technical repetition of some highlighted actions but in a varied environment. Practice length can vary but the below diagram has been conducted using a 10-yard distance from GK1's goal to server 1.

Description: The practice starts with server 1 striking a ball in and around GK1 to handle. GK1 then gives GK2 a diving save (in this practice a high dive) that they will look to secure. GK2 will then roll the ball to server 1 who will advance towards GK1 and try to score in the mini goal.

Diagram:

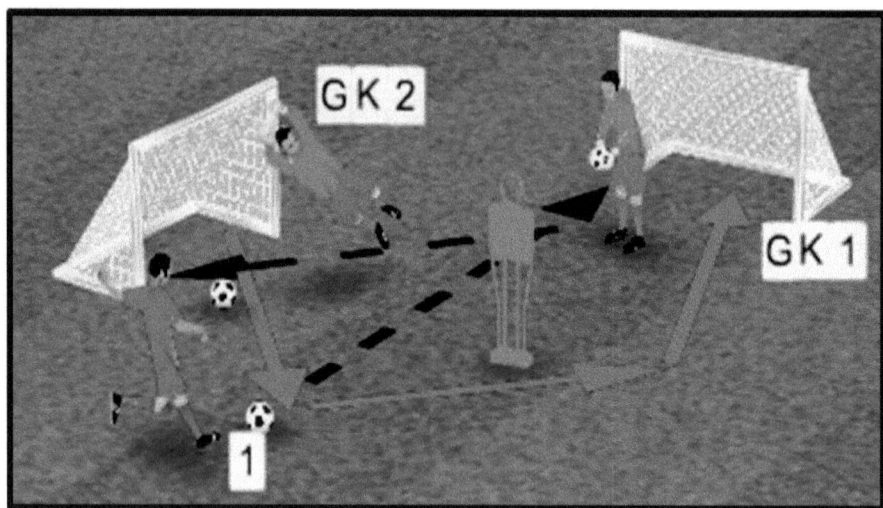

Progressions:

Distances and heights of server 1's strike and the diving save for GK2.

Make goals bigger to challenge the GKs.

Angle of approach from server 1 to GK2 (have a time or touch limit if necessary).

Learning Detail:

Technical: Consistency of handling from GK1 and GK2 in their first serves | 1v1 response from GK2 – make an early judgement on how to save – smother, spread, block or lower limb intervention

Tactical: GK1's timing, intent and approach to engage the ball from server 1

Psychological: Concentration on more foundation-based actions such as general handling, diving fluency, and balance/co-ordination | Decision from GK 1 on when, where, and how to engage the ball or to stay and set | Ability to read the triggers from server 1 as they attack – big touch out of server 1's feet

Physical: Balanced set position from GK1 initially | Diving explosiveness and goal overage from GK 2 | Look for the speed and control of movement from GK1 in the 1v1 situation | Flexibility of lower body and strength of upper body shape during 1v1 phase

Social/Environmental: Acknowledgment of good practice by all GKs to build a high tempo yet challenging practice arena

29

Goalkeeping Themes: 1v1 scenarios and recognising triggers to engage the ball.

Practice Objectives: To provide the GKs with opportunities to practice different types of 1v1 engagements, with a focus on timing and approach towards the ball.

Description: There are three goals on the outside of the playing area, each with balls stationed next to them. The coach will call a number (indicated on the diagram) and this GK will fetch a ball and advance towards any goal to try and score. If the ball stays in the playing area after an initial attempt, the practice will continue. Variations and progressions will be stated below.

Diagram:

Progressions:

GKs on one touch then shoot (varying weight and angle of touch).

Time limit to finish – or no limits of time / touches at all.

Change goal size, ball positioning, and even playing area size.

Instead of a verbal trigger from the coach, use a visual trigger – for example, each goal has a coloured cone by the goal and the coach has these cones next to him; they touch the cone to give that coloured goal the chance to initiate the attack

Learning Detail:

Technical: 1v1 response from GK– make an early judgement on how to save – smother, spread, block or lower limb intervention | Head position when making any saves will be crucial

Tactical: GK's timing, intent and approach to engage the ball from the attacker

Psychological: Decision from GK 1 on when, where and how to engage the ball or to stay and set | Ability to read the triggers from server 1 as they attack – big touch out of server 1's feet | Ability of GK to hold their nerve to delay and not go to ground too easily

Physical: Balance and timing of approach to the ball | Effectiveness to co-ordinate limbs to deflect the ball away | Observe GKs footwork and stride pattern to advance or track the ball side to side

Social/Environmental: Acknowledgment of good practice by all GKs to build a high tempo yet challenging practice arena | Emphasise consistency yet allow the GKs to experiment and try new saving methods

30

Goalkeeping Themes: Randomly positioned attempts on the goal – emphasising goal protection.

Practice Objectives: To allow the GKs to interpret different situations around the penalty box. With an additional focus on deflections, rebounds and responding to loose balls.

Description: There are three different start positions for the ball which will be delivered at server 1's discretion. Both GKs will position themselves in relation to this ball. GK1 has the main goal to protect and GK2 has a smaller goal – 8-10 yards out – marked out by mannequins or poles. Once the ball is played to server 2, they have one touch and strike at either goal. If ball goes past GK2, GK1 should attempt to save the ball as well. The ball is live until dealt with by a GK or has been scored. Server 2 will then travel towards the ball on the right-hand side for a first time strike on goal for GK1 to attempt to save.

Diagram:

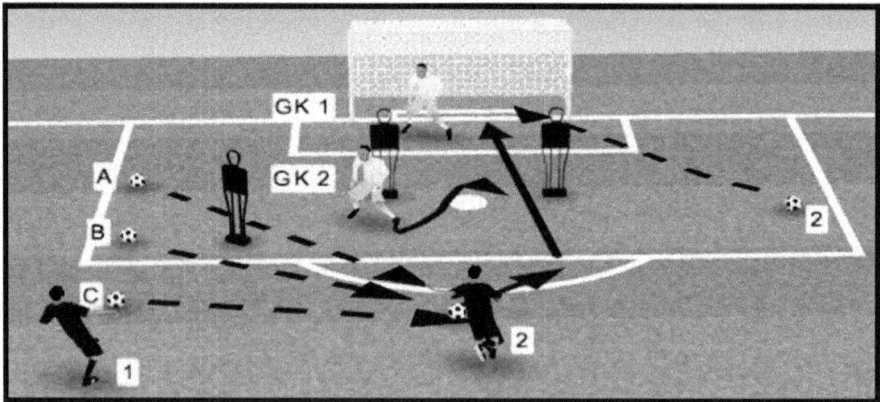

Progressions:

Change the conditions on server 2 and the position of their second strike on goal.

Rotate positions and roles.

Learning Detail:

Technical: If diving, whether to go with 1 or 2 hands | Observations on dive shape and appropriateness (first step, negative dive or shuffle then dive) | Have a look at leg/foot saves in this environment – when and where

Tactical: General positioning in relation to the ball and/or pressure | Observe efficiency of re-positioning from different attempts on goal

Psychological: Response speed to the travel of the ball | Decision making focus on the technical response to defend the goal

Physical: Control and co-ordination in response to server 1's ball movement | Set position for both GKs from the first strike | The ability of GK1 to be flexible and agile enough to change direction from any deflections | GK2's shape if the server comes closer to them | GK2's physical response to the angled strike on goal

Social/Environmental: Acknowledgment of good practice by all GKs to build a high tempo yet challenging practice arena

31

Goalkeeping Themes: Cutbacks into strikes on goal from 14-21 yards.

Practice Objectives: To provide repetition on cutback situations with different angles of shots on goal. The focus will be on re-positioning after the cutback and/or off a touch from the server. Emphasis, from the attacker's viewpoint, on any contact being sharp due to the mannequins replicating a defensive line.

Description: The ball starts with server 1 who starts at different positions outside the box on the wing. They take a touch out of their feet and play the ball into a marked out zone (shaded area, 14-21 yards). Server 2 shoots first time or has a quick touch before shooting. A, B and C indicate the variation of passes from server 1 so angles are different for each attempt on goal. If the ball strikes the mannequins the ball is still live.

Diagram:

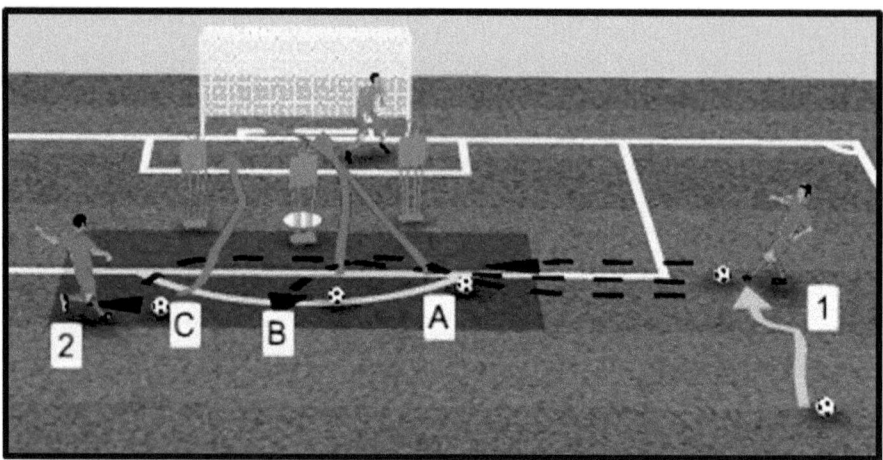

Progressions:

Take constraints off attacker but emphasise quick attempts on goal.

Allow server 1 to cut into the box and play to server 2.

Build in a counter attack situation if the ball is secured by GK.

Learning Detail:

Technical: Ability to respond technically to different heights, speeds, and trajectories of attempts on goal

Tactical: Initial start position in relation to server 1 before the touch – appropriateness | Re-adjustment depending on direction of the pass across | What happens if server 2 takes a touch?

Psychological: Capacity to respond to triggers from either server | Overall decision making of technical response to goal protection

Physical: Stance and balance of set position before initial contact (shot or touch) | Control and co-ordination of travel around the goal mouth | Footwork to move laterally before initiating diving step

Social/Environmental: The strikes on goal need to be realistic – could utilise outfield players or coach striking first to set the tone for the service

32

Goalkeeping Themes: Crossed balls involving reaction saves.

Practice Objectives: To provide the GKs with a variety of crossed balls – lofted, floated, clipped and drilled delivery service. Focus will be on initial decision to come for the ball and how this is dealt with (catch, punch and help on). If not coming, what's the action required? After initial contact, there will be an element of reaction saves that involve the ability to re-position very quickly.

Description: Phase 1 – the ball will start from the crosser, they look to deliver anywhere in the playing zone. The GKs will look to come for the ball or drop back in to defend the goal. If the ball is caught and secured by a GK then Phase 2 will start. If there is another contact (such as a punch away) then the ball will restart from the crosser.

Phase 2 – The GK that claims the ball will retreat back to the goal line and try and score with a volley or half volley in any of the other goals.

Diagram:

Progressions:

Change angle and distance of crosser (as well as them striking a moving ball). Add in mannequins to advance the practice as well.

Add in a second shot on goal from the crosser after either phase.

Learning Detail:

Technical: How the GKs deal with the initial cross | Is the technical response appropriate to the delivered ball | Speed of limbs within phase 2 and ability to hold shape of save from close range attempts

Tactical: Where to drop to defend the goal – observe where the initial contact is coming from and are the GK(s) in the right half of the goal to defend any attempts on goal

Psychological: Speed of decision whether to engage ball or not – hold feet until decision is made | Awareness of other players in the playing area

Physical: The timing and application of jump mechanics | Footwork either towards or backwards from the ball – observe GKs ability to drive through the ball or rotate shoulders backwards | Ability to maintain balance whilst in mid-air and hang time | How the GKs deal with and respond to the physical challenge

Social/Environmental: Be aware of the physicality of this practice and monitor approaches | Emphasis on allowing the GKs to come for the crosses and not being afraid to make mistakes

33

Goalkeeping Themes: Reaction saves from 1-7 yards.

Practice Objectives: To expose the GKs to attempts on goal from a short distance, decreasing reaction times. The focus will be on repelling the ball out of the penalty area, and returning to feet as quickly as possible after an initial saving situation.

Description: The ball starts from the server who will be outside the playing area. They take a touch out of their feet and can strike in any goal they want (there could be a pass into this player if numbers allow). The server also has the option to square pass the ball to the GK in the goal facing them for that GK to try and score in any of the side goals. Play restarts from the server once the ball is finished with. If the ball is loose in the playing area after an initial save, then rebounds from the other two GKs can be had in any of the goals.

Diagram:

Progressions: Change GKs in each of the goals.

Have the start position in-between the other goals.

Learning Detail:

Technical: Focus on hand positioning at all phases (before the ball is moved, during the movement, and upon the moment of contact from the attacker)

Tactical: Initial start position from the server – covering the near post | Re-adjustment depending on the choice of delivery from the server – can they cut out or engage the ball?

Psychological: How quickly the GKs can assess what the server will do with the ball | Desire not to be beaten, developing a strong and determined mindset (due to the nature of the practice there will be goals scored) | The choice of the response to save the ball – is it appropriate and effective in that situation?

Physical: Look for the co-ordination and balance of passes across the goal – is the GK set or do they not have time to set? | Emphasise the need for agility and spring from a short distance as there won't usually be time to shift feet after the shot on goal is taken | The ability of the GKs to return to feet is important – do they go straight to smother the ball? Up to set and make a save? Retreat to defend the goal?

Social/Environmental: Allow GKs to challenge each other and set high standards of application – go for every ball and don't give up in any situation

34

Goalkeeping Themes: Multiple technical outcomes – basic handling, first touch, driven pass work, and shot-stopping variations.

Practice Objectives: To test the GK's consistency of linking actions together along with repetition on some technical and physical foundations. The actions and areas of focus in this practice can be altered to change the objectives – e.g. server 1 in this practice can test the GK on whatever the coach sees fit.

Description: The ball starts with server 1 who gives the GK a scoop save at a firm pace. The ball is rolled back to server 1. The GK then moves to receive a pass from server 2 (at this point, look at support positions for the ball). The GK will take one touch and drive the ball back towards the goal of server 2 – server 2 will try and save this ball. The GK will then travel across the goal to server 3, who'll take a touch either side of the mannequin and try to score against the GK.

Diagram:

Progressions:

Variation of server 1's delivery.

The ball the GK scoops from server 1 can be rolled to server 2 which will initiate their pass.

Move the goal of server 2 to create different angles and distances.

Change the position of server 3.

Learning Detail:

Technical: Look at the variations and leg positioning of the scoop save | The ability of the GK to drive the ball – using laces and fluid kicking action | Although server 2 is not the focus – emphasise their role in saving the driven pass | Effectiveness of the technical response to server 3's attempt

Tactical: The re-positioning of the GK from servers 2 to 3 for the attempt on goal – think staying deep before advancing towards the ball to give more response time

Psychological: Concentration throughout the practice phases | Ability to adapt to the changing movement of the ball | Re-enforce the need for consistency with the GK in all phases of the practice

Physical: Observe the general co-ordination and control between all actions – especially the passing phase | How the GK travels back across the goal – stride patterns and arm movement; and think about the distance they're travelling – does their movement allow them to travel quickly but then decelerate back into set position?

Social/Environmental: The accuracy and consistency of the serving in this practice will dictate, to a large extent, how challenging it is for the GK

35

Goalkeeping Themes: Diving saves, incorporating the decision to set before the dive or not.

Practice Objectives: To allow the GK to build confidence and analyse situations when there is a need to set and leg drive for a diving action, or to carry on running through to generate momentum in the dive. There will be different start points in the practice but the first action will be to protect a mannequin from being hit or 'protect your mate'.

Description: Phase 1 – the balls start with server 1 or 2. The coach or non-working GK will call either 1 or 2 and, at this point, the server will take a touch and look to hit their adjacent mannequin. The GK at the point of touch will travel across and look to protect the mannequin.

Phase 2 – once phase 1 has been completed and regardless of the outcome – the non-working GK will move into the goal and receive a strike on goal from the server that didn't strike in phase 1. If the GK secures this ball, they distribute back to the other server who took the shot in phase 1.

Diagrams:

Progressions: Change the distance of the servers – closer to challenge or further away to regress to give the GK more time to assess the ball.

Have a moving ball from the second server – or another situation (1v1 for instance).

Learning Detail:

Technical: How GK1 goes about best protecting the mannequin | Response from GK2 in relation to the situation they are faced with

Tactical: No real tactical element here apart from the positioning of each GK in their phases – if distribution is incorporated within phase 2, look at the playability of their passes | The depth of server 2 if there are mannequins in their direct vicinity – the GK would drop to give themselves more reaction time

Psychological: Speed of assessment and then execution from GK1 in their phase | Desire to protect their mate! | The awareness of different weights and directions of touch from servers and how this impacts their positioning and physical movements

Physical: In phase 1, does the GK need to set or can they produce a diving action whilst travelling in the same direction? Focus on momentum and dive coverage | General agility and flexibility in all actions from both GKs to manipulate their body to best affect the ball | Set position of GK for a longer range attempt – in order for them to shift their feet quickly

Social/Environmental: High energy and enthusiasm in this practice – GKs set the tone with their application and willingness to produce fast and agile actions at all times

36

Goalkeeping Themes: Crossing scenarios involving distribution.

Practice Objectives: To provide the GKs with some challenges and high-pressure scenarios in a tight crossing area where they can build confidence in coming for the ball and withstand a physical challenge. Think about the ages of the GKs here – factor in goal size and distances from the crosser.

Description: The ball starts from server 1 who delivers the ball into the designated playing area for either GK1 or GK2 to come and affect the ball. The striker in the vicinity can try and score in any goal. If GK1 secures the ball, they take the ball to the side of the goal and look to play to the target player; wherever they are, GK1 needs to select the most appropriate distribution method to enable the server to secure the ball. The server will deliver balls from different angles and distances with the GKs switching goals every 10 crosses to get an opportunity to work on their distribution.

Diagram:

Progressions:

Alter the playing area in terms of size – bigger distances in-between goals for a different picture.

Change the crossing sides and have a touch before delivery from the server.

Server delivers with left and right foot to give GKs experience of different starting positions.

Learning Detail:

Technical: Response to the cross – catch, punch or help on with emphasis on hand shape and the timing of this action | Distribution action – focus on this as a separate part depending on what GK is focusing on (GKs can be working on different methods in the same practice)

Tactical: Initial start position in relation to the ball – left or right foot? Distance and angle? | If the GK is not coming towards the ball, do they position themselves accordingly, in relation to the first contact from the ball?

Psychological: The assessment of the ball initially and if the GK can affect the ball or not | Main decisions include how to deal with the cross or attempt on goal and how to respond to the specific crossing scenario

Physical: Ability to generate height and power of jump from standing start | Getting momentum through the ball to punch | Withstand physical contact and keep balance/control of the body (including landing technique)

Social/Environmental: Encourage physical contact in controlled manner (depends on ages of GKs)

37

Goalkeeping Themes: Quick shooting and general shot-stopping save selection.

Practice Objectives: To expose the GK to various types of attempts on goal from different angles and distances and allow them to select the best and most appropriate technical response to that attempt.

Description: There a number of servers (other GKs) in a fixed sized box who are given a number; they are performing ball manipulation tasks with their hands (bounces etc.). When a number is called, that server will move out of the grid, throw the ball to the coach who has a rebound net in their hands (or a pass back if not available) and will play the ball back into the path of this server. The server will either shoot first time or take a touch and shoot on goal. No matter the outcome, this server will take the place in goal of the defending GK, with the GK using that server's ball and making their way to the box. The process will then start again.

Diagram:

Progressions:

Move the box away from a central position.

Add mannequins to the attempt on goal phase.

Instead of a rotation after the attempt on goal – the GK defending the goal stays in until they concede.

Learning Detail:

Technical: Give the GKs in the box specific technical objectives to improve their ball manipulation/handling skills | the emphasis will be on save selection and how the GK responds to the attempt on goal – focus on their individual technically styles and effectiveness

Tactical: No major tactical focus apart from GK's positioning from the server's one-two, or first touch

Psychological: GK's concentration before server advances and their ability to read the server's movements | Response of the GK in terms of their goal protection

Physical: Set position balance and 'readiness' before attempts on goal

Social/Environmental: Allow the GKs to experiment with different techniques and if the practice develops into a progression of staying to defend the goal until scored against – emphasise this never beaten mentality

38

Goalkeeping Themes: How the GKs defend their goals based upon the specific scenario that they are faced with – with a focus on parry/deflection areas.

Practice Objectives: To replicate a random and varied environment where the entry points from servers are ever-changing and the servers are under different constraints. The distance from the zone to the goals can change based upon specific objectives (short range or long range attempts on goal).

Description: There are GKs defending goals (two shown here) and a zone where a number of GKs are throwing the ball to each other to practice handling and footwork. These GKs are numbered and from the call of the coach, that designated numbered server recovers the ball, rolls out of the zone at any angle and distance of roll they want, and strikes the ball at any goal they choose. If the GK secures the ball, they will distribute back into the zone. If the ball is loose in the playing area from a GK's contact then the server or coach can attempt rebounds in either goal.

Diagram:

Progressions:

Make the goal that the GKs will defend different sizes, e.g. 9-a-side and 11-a-side goals.

Vary the distances of the goal from the zone and the positioning of the goals.

The server who is shooting can play a one-two pass with the coach before their attempt on goal.

Learning Detail:

Technical: If defending the goal – observe when it is best to use leg saves | Can the GK generate or use the pace on the ball to manoeuvre the ball away from the immediate playing area to avoid rebounds

Tactical: Ability to change position depending on the angle of the server's roll out or first touch | The key message is not to be caught in-between defending the goal or defending the space

Psychological: Select where and how to protect the goal | Have a proactive attitude and be positive in all decisions | Focus on the zone where servers are placed – see if the GK can anticipate attacks

Physical: Proficiency in covering the space between the goal and the zone when necessary | General reactive agility in all saving actions | Maintaining shape and not going down too early or easily

Social/Environmental: Rotate GKs every 10 attempts on goal – emphasis on not conceding

39

Goalkeeping Themes: Angled shot-stopping and a focus on parry/deflection areas; there will be opportunities for recovery and reaction saves in some progressions as well.

Practice Objectives: To set the scene for angled shot-stopping in a multipurpose environment. Recovery and reaction saves will be built in at different points.

Description: Phase 1 – servers 1 and 2 have a football and the coach will call either server's number and they will then shoot on goal (this trigger can be replaced with a visual trigger or server touching the ball out of their feet to start the practice). Straight after this attempt, the other server will shoot at the other goal.

Phase 2 – if the ball is loose in the area from the saving GK's first contact, the opposite GK can shoot at the goal to bring in recovery situations. An alternative is that the server (called by the coach) passes across to the opposite server who then shoots at goal.

Diagram:

Progressions:

If GK1 secures the ball (for example) they can then volley the ball straight back to GK2's goal to try and score.

Change the sides and distances of strikers and the positioning of the goals.

If four GKs are working then rotate working GKs and servers at the coach's discretion.

GKs start by facing the ball or facing each other centrally.

Servers shoot stationary or moving balls.

Learning Detail:

Technical: Response to shots on goal looking at the GK's ability to manoeuvre the ball away from immediate danger | When, where and how to utilise leg saves in the practice | For higher attempts on goal, look at top hand vs bottom hand saves and whether using one or two hands is most appropriate in any given situation

Tactical: Apart from initial positioning (depth vs down the line) there is no major tactical element

Psychological: Speed in response to the shot on goal and the selection of the right technique to protect the goal | Positive and aggressive approach to not being beaten | Awareness of any rebound or recovery save situations and the focus within

Physical: Strength and power of one step dives to cover the goal and gain momentum into the movement | The co-ordination behind how the GK gets off the ground after an initial diving action

Social/Environmental: Quality and consistency of shots on goal | Observe if practice needs to be progressed or regressed

40

Goalkeeping Themes: Vision and awareness within shooting situations and general goal protection.

Practice Objectives: To enhance the ability of the GK to respond to different angles of approach from an attacker. The servers in this practice will be moving which will create an air of chaos. There can be distribution and recovery save elements built into this practice.

Description: There is one working GK with numbered servers in a playing area (area shown 20x20 yard grid). These servers are travelling around in front of the mannequins with a ball each. Two mannequins will also be placed 8 yards in front of the GK to obscure vision and alter positioning. Either the working GK or a resting GK (internally or externally paced tempo of shot-stopping) will call a number – wherever that server is positioned, they will take a varied touch and shoot on goal to try and score. The working GK can stay in for a designated number of shots on goal or rotate. If the ball is loose in the playing area, rebounds can be had on goal.

Diagram:

Progressions:

If GK secures the ball, they distribute accurately back to the server who had the shot on goal.

Change playing area size and distance of mannequins from the goal.

Work on 1v1 situations in this same practice design.

Learning Detail:

Technical: Save selection and technical response to the first shot on goal | This practice can be used to get some good work around the notion of catch, parry or deflect the ball

Tactical: Initial start position in the goal mouth | Moving into an appropriate position for that GK (not the same position for everyone and depends on certain GK styles and philosophies)

Psychological: Ability to track the ball as best as possible from the server and through the mannequins | If defending the goal for a longer period of time, concentration and attention will need to be of a high level

Physical: General balance and co-ordination of set position | Showing agility and extension of arms in order to reach balls further away from the midline of the body | It would be a good idea to use bigger goals than a GK might be used to, for working on footwork for diving saves and goal coverage

Social/Environmental: Focus on the servers using the whole grid to travel around in, so shots on goal are also from a different angle and the weight of initial 1st touch is varied to change distances between GK and the ball

41

Goalkeeping Themes: Handling situations (with dive actions and reaction saves).

Practice Objectives: To give GKs exposure to different handling situations within different types of attempts on goal.

Description: Server 1 starts with the ball and gives GK1 a dive action (random or pre-determined height/distance). GK1 throws from the floor back to server 1 and returns to feet as soon as possible to travel cross to server 2. Server 2 will take a touch (varied) around the opposite stationary player as soon as GK1 is on their feet and try to score. If GK1 secures server 2's ball, then they take two steps and volley the ball at GK2's goal to try and score.

Diagram:

Progressions:

Have server 1's dive move in the same direction as server 2's side – replicate a recovery save.

Change the angle and distance from goal of server 2 (depending on what types of save are being worked on (long distance, reactions etc.).

Change the distance of GK2's goal from the main goal area worked in.

Vary GK1's service if they secure the ball (e.g. drop and drive or throwing method).

Learning Detail:

Technical: GK1's dive mechanics (a chance to work on technique here) | GK1's response to the attempt on goal – is their choice of technique appropriate? | GK2's ability to keep shape from attempts struck hard or from close range

Tactical: GK1 looks to travel deep at first to give them more reaction time rather than going directly towards the ball

Psychological: | Recognise the triggers to set during GK1's travel movement | Decision on how to respond to the strike from server 2 – potentially based upon GK's positioning, efficiency of travel, and their balance/co-ordination while travelling

Physical: The main focus needs to be on where and when GK1 will decelerate and set whilst travelling from server 1 to server 2 – the service from 2 will come at intermittent times so this is unpredictable

Social/Environmental: Highlight key objectives for each GK before the start of the practice

42

Goalkeeping Themes: General handling and an emphasis on when and where to set (focus on deceleration and balance).

Practice Objectives: To provide the GK with repetition of handling opportunities – ideal for a warm up as there will different movement patterns available. The main objective (as well as the technical information) is to identify when to set from server 2.

Description: Server 1 is in a 6x6 grid moving around with a ball presented in their hands. On the shout (can be a visual trigger) of the server/coach, the working GK travels to wherever server 1 is located and touches the ball then moves back across the goal to an effective and appropriate position for server 2's ball.

Diagram:

Progressions:

Server 2's striking position can vary depending on each GK's individual focus – they can move after the trigger as well, so the GK needs to be aware of a new position.

Addition of mannequins or a second server.

Change position of grid – move in towards the goal.

Learning Detail:

Technical: Specific handling observations – where is the GK catching the ball in relation to the body? Is the response to the ball the best option to use in that given scenario?

Tactical: The position back from the ball to the goal will depend on the positioning of server 2's ball

Psychological: Vision and awareness of the situation the GK finds themselves in | Decision making speed in the technical/physical response | Have the confidence and bravery to try new techniques and allow the GK to find out what is effective for them

Physical: Stride patterns of the movement from the ball back to the goal are | Cross-over step vs sidestep? – treat each GK as an individual due to body shape, size, and co-ordination | Head position on the secondary travel from ball – scanning and assessing the situation

Social/Environmental: A focus on consistency of technical actions | Use as a chance for a GK to work on their passing and ball striking by having them as server 2

43

Goalkeeping Themes: Different types of passes from varying angles – with focus on the GK's initial support position, body shape and ball connection.

Practice Objectives: To allow repetitive focused work on different passing techniques and give the GK exposure to receiving the ball from different positions and hitting different target areas.

Description: There can be one or two working GKs – the ball will be played in from a set position (A or B); the GK will look to play off two touches to strike towards the goal. The GK can position themselves in different positions indicated by the numbers outside the penalty area.

Depending on what range of passing is focused on will dictate how far the GK starts – for example if working on a longer range, clip the start 25+ yards back. This practice can be structured in many different ways with GKs having a set number of passes

Diagram:

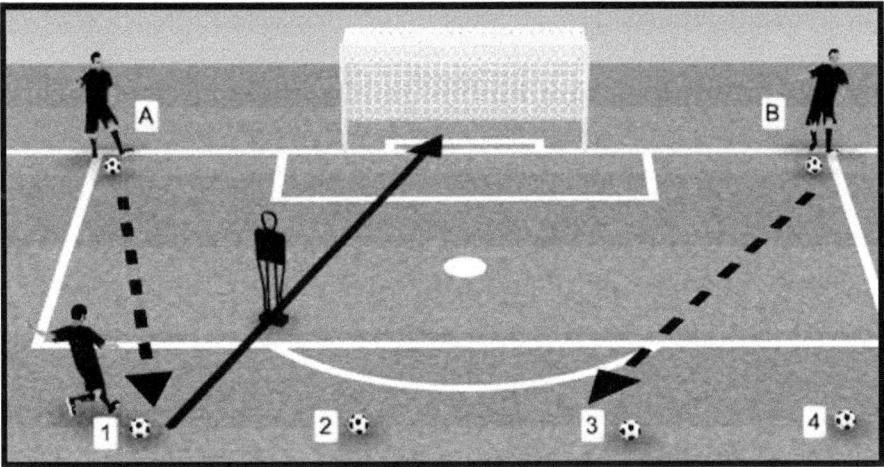

Progressions:

If working with GKs on driven passes, have a GK defending the goal to build in some obstacles and shot-stopping for this GK.

Add pressure to the receiving GK so they can start to work on supporting with different types of pressure as this will effect where they place themselves.

Learning Detail:

Technical: Major focus on first touch and ball striking technique – each GK will have a slightly different approach although the fundamentals will stay the same

Tactical: Pass selection is a detail to select the best option given the target player or distance – making the ball playable to the receiving player or to the target zone

Psychological: Decision of where the first touch is taken in relation to the GK's body to allow them to get the best possible connection based upon the technical selection

Physical: Balance and co-ordination when moving into position, first touch and ball contact | Open body shape to receive, which opens up the pitch | Striking through the ball (listen to the connection)

Social/Environmental: Keep the environment varied for higher ability GKs as once they've gained a good level of technical prowess the next steps are to select the best pass in different situations

44

Goalkeeping Themes: Through balls – recognition to defend the space or defend the goal.

Practice Objectives: To give GKs opportunities to work on recognising when they can engage the ball and to work on various 1v1 saving techniques. Servers will start anywhere behind the mannequins to advance onto the ball.

Description: The ball starts with server 1 who takes a touch out of their feet and plays either around or through the mannequins for either server 2 or 3. This pass can be to feet or space. The servers will have one touch to try and score (this can be a time limit before an attempt, or playing live until the ball is secure or out of the playing area).

If the GK secures the ball, they distribute back to server 1. If the ball stays in the playing area from a save by the GK, both servers are allowed to attempt a first touch rebound.

Diagram:

Progressions:

Have a pass into server 1 to give the GK a new starting position.

Server 1 can work along the width of the box – central or angled ball entries.

Learning Detail:

Technical: Response to the situation if the server has the ball under control – stay big and delay | Does the GK need to block, spread or smother?

Tactical: Initial start position and stance in relation to the ball (front foot) | Change of position based upon the angle and weight of the pass to be in a position to pro-actively defend the space in front

Psychological: Ability to recognise the through ball's characteristics (pace, direction, height) and the decision of when and how to engage | Bravery to leave the goal and also to put one's body in physically dangerous positions

Physical: Speed and control in travelling to engage the ball (look at acceleration and deceleration) | Pay attention to head position on 1v1 engagements | Movement adaptability – change direction and have the physical capacity and capability to cover ground whilst maintaining body control/balance

Social/Environmental: Put the focus on the GK's (and not the server's) role in scoring goals – but emphasise (due to the specific situation worked on) that there will be goals scored in this practice

45

Goalkeeping Themes: Balls across the face of the goalmouth - involving reaction saves and goal protection.

Practice Objectives: To work on the ability of the GK to recognise when they can look to cut out the ball, when to drop back to defend the ball, and when to engage the ball off an initial touch close into the goalmouth from an attacker. Attempts on goal can be volleys, headers or basic finishes.

Description: The ball starts from server 1 who can throw the ball in or drop/side volley the ball into the playing area. The emphasis will be on the server to vary heights, pace and directions of this delivery. Server 2 is on a first time finish and server 3 is allowed to take one touch before a strike (but this needs to be sharp to replicate the fact that they will be closed down quickly being in this position). Both servers are looking to score from the outset.

Diagram:

Progressions:

Change the delivery position of server 1.

Play rebounds off an initial save.

Add different runs from attacking servers or build in a live defender to the practice.

Learning Detail:

Technical: Body and limbs to keep ball out – how is this done? | Speed of technical assessment

Tactical: Starting position and attitude/body language for server 1's delivery | If GK can't affect the ball (because of height or placement), take up a position based upon the anticipated first contact of attacking servers

Psychological: Assessment of delivered ball – is there enough time to cover the distance to affect the ball? | Bravery to make an initial contact when the ball is delivered into the 6 yard box | Desire and commitment to not be beaten along with attitude/application if goals are being scored

Physical: Body shape if engaging the ball | Strength to repel the ball and withstand contact | Set position analysis to allow GK to generate power from a one-step dive if the ball is struck with pace

Social/Environmental: Challenging situation for the GK so be realistic with what success will be; for example, if the GK makes a very good block but comes back out towards the server – is this an error? Or in a match would the team's defence clear this ball?

46

Goalkeeping Themes: Handling, goalmouth travel techniques and fundamental shot-stopping principles.

Practice Objectives: To enhance the ability of GKs to maintain body control during movement across the ball and being in a solid and steady position in order to make saves.

Description: There are two working GKs. On the call of 'Go', GKs1 and 2 will receive strikes in and around their body from both servers 1. They will then travel across the goal for another strike from servers 1. This strike can be stationary or a moving ball. After this phase, GK1 will move into a central position and receive a strike to score from server 3. If the ball is still live in the area then first touch rebounds are available from any server. GK2 will then repeat this process. GKs can swap after one set each or stay in for a pre-determined number of sets (the number of serves).

Diagram:

Progressions:

Change angles and distances of the two servers at 1 (mix up with left and right foot servers as well).

Server 3 needs a touch around the mannequin to shoot – this could be a 1v1 on a pass to a server 1 for a strike on goal.

Learning Detail:

Technical: Ability to deal with each ball on its own individual merits | Recovery saves focus on server 3 – can the GK select the right response?

Tactical: When travelling on the angle – don't overcompensate at the front post | Adaptable positioning from server 3 as this will be a quick shift around the mannequin

Psychological: Concentration on the fundamentals – don't lose the basics in this practice | Ability to process the triggers and factors in server 3's picture – there will be bodies around the playing area

Physical: Ability to decelerate into the set position – decreasing stride length after travelling across the goal | General speed and agility in protecting the goal from server 3

Social/Environmental: High tempo, high intensity and high consistency – use this practice for GKs to challenge each other and set a really good standard

47

Goalkeeping Themes: Technical response and selection of actions –
decision making process in a high pace environment.

Practice Objectives: To utilise multiple goals and prepare the GKs to
the high-paced and creative nature of attempts on goal from this region of
the pitch.

Description: The server starts on ball A which is struck in and around
the GK for a catch – if this is spilled out, the practice will restart. Once
the ball is secure, the GK will look to score in either mini goal – start with
throwing then build up to drop and drive or full volleys. If the ball comes
back off either GK2 or GK3, GK1 can rebound first time on any goal.
Once this phase is complete, the server will strike ball B at GK1 and try to
score. Again, if GK1 secures the ball then they can try and score in the
mini goals again.

Diagram:

Progressions:

Balls A and B can change position and be moving when struck.

Rotate GKs in the goals – make a competition as well to create an emphasis on goal protection.

Learning Detail:

Technical: Catching techniques (scoop, cup or 'W' shapes) | GK2 and GK3 to maintain shape in order to deflect and repel the ball in front of their goals | Distribution methods of GK1, make sure they don't rush and strike/throw balls without stable balance

Tactical: No major tactical element apart from GK1's change in position to face ball B – do they drop into line first to give themselves more time?

Psychological: Speed of technical response and decision based upon the picture faced on how to save the ball | Although catching the ball is a focus – work with the GK on the factors behind whether they can catch the ball or not (pace, height, spin/turn, bounce and surface for example)

Physical: Ability of all GKs to set to give themselves enough time to move efficiently and fluently towards the ball

Social/Environmental: Speed of distribution from GK1 is paramount | Emphasise consistency in catching when possible but to respond to each ball on its own merits

48

Goalkeeping Themes: Blocking techniques – designed to build confidence and introduce the technique.

Practice Objectives: To work on the physical elements of the GK blocking the ball. Also provides a focus on the timing behind approaching the ball whilst working on the basics of these blocking techniques.

Description: GK will start in a goal with four balls in front of them (3-4 yards) with server 1 starting the same distance opposite the balls. When server 1 travels to a ball, the GK will follow the server to this ball and make a blocking save.

Diagram:

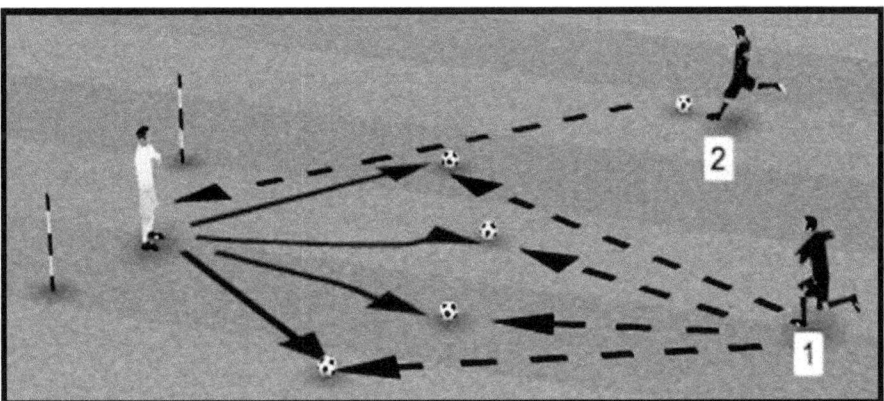

Progressions:

After an initial blocked save from server 1, GKs drops back to the goal for a strike from server 2 – this looks to replicate the ball bouncing off the GK to another player.

Change distances of balls and server 1.

If server 1 gets to a ball first, they can then look to shoot straight away or go around the GK to change the picture.

Learning Detail:

Technical: Links closely to the physical detail – focus on limb position and technical selection if the ball changes direction or the picture changes (attacker has control or the ball is lost)

Tactical: Approach direct to the ball (Ball, Body, Goal) | Ability to respond to second ball – recovery save or recovery line to the goal | Positioning in relation to server 3's ball if applicable

Psychological: Not to be afraid to engage the ball when attacker is coming at speed or to let the ball hit the body – can use softer balls for repetitive practices | Awareness to track server and have a fast response time

Physical: Lower limb flexibility to get into a low body shape | Head over the ball with arms sweeping through in a strong, wide position | Tense body to act as a wall (don't just let the ball hit the GK); a stronger body will mean the blocked ball will go further away from the danger area

Social/Environmental: Allow GKs to experiment with unique styles whilst focusing on the fundamentals

49

Goalkeeping Themes: 1v1 techniques and defending the space in front of a goal.

Practice Objectives: To focus on the GK's ability to cover the space in front of them and defend the goal using 1v1 techniques whilst showing physical adaptability.

Description: Servers 1 and 2 are playing the ball to each other 6 yards apart. At any point, server 2 can take the ball either side and attempt to score against either GK in the side goals. They can also let the ball run past them (no touch turn) and attempt to score in the full size goal. Also, server 1 can touch the ball either side of server 2 to strike at the full size goal. The ball is in play until it leaves the playing area or a goal is scored.

Diagram:

Progressions:

GKs rotate goals after a pre-determined number of attempts on goal.

Change goal and server positions.

Learning Detail:

Technical: Select the most effective technical response to the situation faced | Emphasise head positioning in all 1v1 saving situations | Allow the GKs to experiment and find their own effective way to defend the goals

Tactical: Observe each GK's initial positioning and ability to approach the ball in the best possible way for each situation

Psychological: Focus throughout each practice on repetition and movement of the ball | Capacity to read triggers to engage the ball and also servers' body shape/stance

Physical: Timing of the approach to engage server 2 | Ability to manoeuvre body and be flexible enough to adapt to quick changes of the ball | Maintain a strong saving shape in all actions

Social/Environmental: Create a high tempo, challenging and hard-working ethos – take pleasure in defending the goal

50

Goalkeeping Themes: Reaction saves and balls delivered across the penalty area.

Practice Objectives: To develop the GK to respond to crossed balls into the penalty area. Focuses on positioning in relation to the first contact of server 1, the ability to respond and move quickly to defend the goal, and works on set position/body stance to give the GK the best possible foundations to save the ball.

Description: There are two servers opposite a rebound board, each with a ball. Triggers can vary but they include: a call to which server will pass, a touch from either server to initiate practice, the coach behind the goal pointing to which server will initiate the practice. The ball will be played against the rebound board into the path of server 2 who will have a first time attempt on goal. Server 2 could also be on two touches to work on a 1v1 focus with the GK. If with a group of GKs, then roles would be swapped.

Diagram:

Progressions:

Have a second attempt from server 1 who didn't play against the rebound board.

Server 1 plays straight into server 2 for a first or second time attempt on goal.

Learning Detail:

Technical: Handling in relation to the ball | When to use foot saves? | Looking for the GK to show different techniques to adapt to the varying types of attempts on goal

Tactical: No main tactical element apart from the GK's skill in being in the best position (height vs depth in relation to the goal line) from the travelling of the ball from the rebound board

Psychological: Speed of decision making in saving response | Capacity to pick up the flight, path and trajectory of the ball and respond accordingly

Physical: Being in a set position that will allow for optimum movement and power generation | Overall co-ordination in upper and lower body limbs – fast hands and feet | Ability to use body to repel and deflect the ball away from playing area and servers

Social/Environmental: Emphasis on consistency with the servers playing the right passes and making the GK work each time

Other Coaching Books from Bennion Kearny

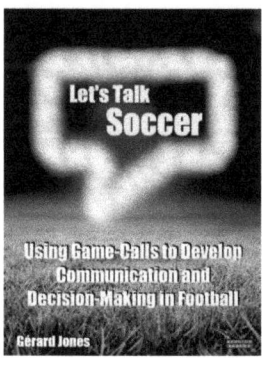

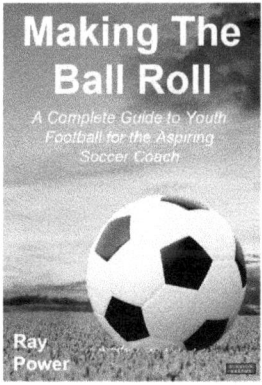

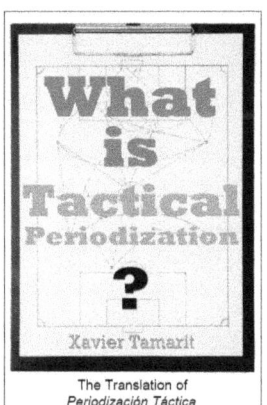

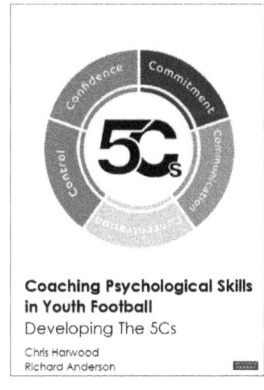

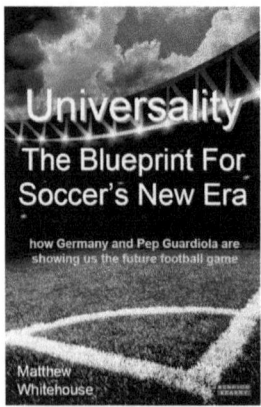

Lightning Source UK Ltd.
Milton Keynes UK
UKHW020620150419
341045UK00014B/1222/P

9 781910 773574